The Second Book of the
LAMBRETTA

www.VelocePress.com

THE LAMBRETTA GRAND PRIX "FORMULA 150"

THE LAMBRETTA SX 150

The Second Book of the
LAMBRETTA
ALL LI AND TV MODELS
FROM 1957

R. H. WARRING

ANNOUNCEMENT

By special arrangement with the original publishers of this book, Sir Isaac Pitman & Son, Ltd., of London, England, we have secured the exclusive publishing rights for this book, as well as all others in THE MOTORCYCLIST'S LIBRARY.

Included in THE MOTORCYCLIST'S LIBRARY are complete instruction manuals covering the care and operation of respective motorcycles and engines; valuable data on speed tuning, and thrilling accounts of motorcycle race events. See listing of available titles elsewhere in this edition.

We consider it a privilege to be able to offer so many fine titles to our customers.

FLOYD CLYMER
Publisher of Books Pertaining to Automobiles and Motorcycles

2125 W. PICO ST.   LOS ANGELES 6, CALIF.

INTRODUCTION

Welcome to the world of digital publishing ~ the book you now hold in your hand, while unchanged from the original edition, was printed using the latest state of the art digital technology. The advent of print-on-demand has forever changed the publishing process, never has information been so accessible and it is our hope that this book serves your informational needs for years to come. If this is your first exposure to digital publishing, we hope that you are pleased with the results. Many more titles of interest to the classic automobile and motorcycle enthusiast, collector and restorer are available via our website at www.VelocePress.com. We hope that you find this title as interesting as we do.

NOTE FROM THE PUBLISHER

The information presented is true and complete to the best of our knowledge. All recommendations are made without any guarantees on the part of the author or the publisher, who also disclaim all liability incurred with the use of this information.

TRADEMARKS

We recognize that some words, model names and designations, for example, mentioned herein are the property of the trademark holder. We use them for identification purposes only. This is not an official publication.

INFORMATION ON THE USE OF THIS PUBLICATION

This manual is an invaluable resource for the classic motorcycle enthusiast and a "must have" for owners interested in performing their own maintenance. However, in today's information age we are constantly subject to changes in common practice, new technology, availability of improved materials and increased awareness of chemical toxicity. As such, it is advised that the user consult with an experienced professional prior to undertaking any procedure described herein. While every care has been taken to ensure correctness of information, it is obviously not possible to guarantee complete freedom from errors or omissions or to accept liability arising from such errors or omissions. Therefore, any individual that uses the information contained within, or elects to perform or participate in do-it-yourself repairs or modifications acknowledges that there is a risk factor involved and that the publisher or its associates cannot be held responsible for personal injury or property damage resulting from the use of the information or the outcome of such procedures.

WARNING!

One final word of advice, this publication is intended to be used as a reference guide, and when in doubt the reader should consult with a qualified technician.

Preface

THE Lambretta motor scooter is highly esteemed, and rightly so because of its technical excellence and general reliability. All Lambretta models and spares are manufactured in Italy and imported into this country by Lambretta Concessionaires Limited, Lambretta House, Purley Way, Croydon, Surrey. A nation-wide service to Lambretta owners is offered via numerous distributors throughout the country, so that the Lambretta owner should never be far from a source of spares or service. This, in fact, applies almost equally throughout Europe. The Lambretta Authorised Service Dealers set-up is amongst the finest of its kind in the world and has been established for some fifteen years.

When this book was first written the text was based on the then current Series I models, and was expanded in detail in later editions to cover the Series II models. Since then several intermediate designs have appeared, culminating in standardization of production of three Series III models (1970). In the preparation of this fourth edition a decision had to be made whether to concentrate on later models to the exclusion of earlier types or to attempt to cover the whole production range through from 1957. It was decided that the latter would be the most useful treatment since the general engineering characteristics have followed the same "Lambretta family" pattern throughout, and thus maintenance, routine servicing, and even disassembly and reassembly follow a similar pattern, although there may be minor differences involved. This leaves the largely unchanged original text as probably the only detailed reference readily available for the servicing of older models, whilst descriptions of specific modifications which have occurred in later productions are included where appropriate. Particular note should be taken of production modifications as these can affect the choice and suitability of spares, since in most cases spares available are of later or current production time.

It is hoped that by this treatment all owners of Lambrettas from the Series I models of 1957 through to the current Series III machines, except mopeds, will find the technical points they need covered, as well as necessary routine servicing and maintenance details.

R. H. W.

THE LAMBRETTA J 125

THE LAMBRETTA 75 C.C. VEGA—A MOPED RATHER THAN A SCOOTER

Contents

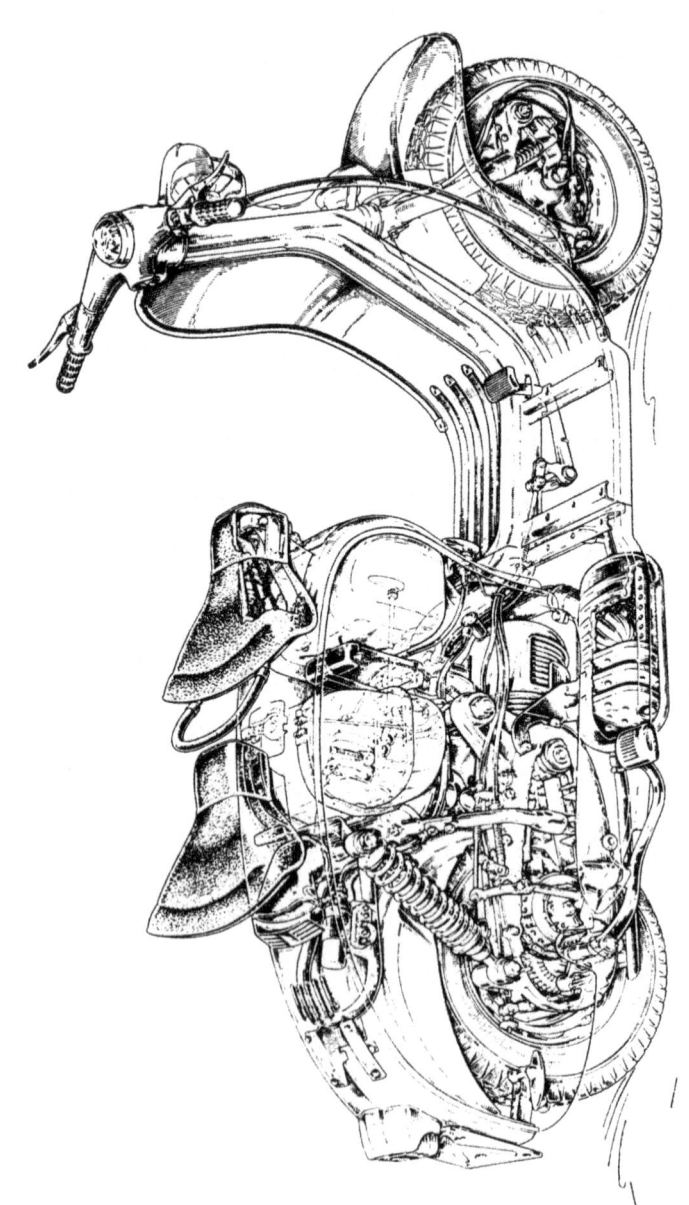

FIG. 1. CUT-AWAY VIEW OF SERIES I LI MODEL

1 Lambretta Models 1952–1970

THE first Lambretta motor-scooters produced in Italy after the war (Models A and B) featured a 123 c.c. engine on a central-girder frame, with double tubes bent around the tank and over the engine, supporting the seats. Model C, introduced in 1952, incorporated a single-tube frame and the back wheel sprung independently of the transmission case. Model D, which appeared later, used torsion-bar rear suspension in which the whole engine-transmission unit was pivotally mounted. With the introduction of Model D, two engine sizes were made available—125 c.c. and 150 c.c. —and from 1955 the 150 c.c. D and LD models have been imported into this country. The 125 LD Mk. III was introduced in 1957 and the 125 LD Mk. IV in 1959. LC and LD models are equivalent to the corresponding C and D models with the addition of engine covers and more protective fairing. Complete details of all these models are given in the companion volume, *The First Book of the Lambretta*.

The Lambretta Tv and Li models represent a complete change in design and are different throughout. They are the result of some twelve years' research and experience in scooter production, the aim being to produce a machine which requires considerably less attention to maintenance and to improve ease of access to all points and components which may need attention. At the same time suspension, stability and braking have also been improved and the styling generally refined. The engine is entirely new and the original shaft transmission with three-speed gearbox and primary bevel drive has been replaced by a Duplex chain drive to a four-speed gearbox mounted on the rear axle. A kick-starter is standard, acting against ratchet mechanism at the output sprocket so that, unlike earlier models, the engine cannot be cranked when a gear is engaged, since the clutch does not disengage the kick-starter from the output. Other proven features of Lambretta practice have been retained such as twin trailing-arm front suspension and pivotal mounting of the whole engine-transmission unit, which carries the rear wheel. Wheel sizes have been increased, and wheels are a little narrower, contributing to improved stability.

The Tv 175 was introduced in February, 1958, general appearance being as shown in Fig. 2. The single-cylinder 170 c.c. two-stroke engine is mounted horizontally with the cylinder facing forward, the crankshaft running at right-angles to the frame. Forced draught is provided by fan blades on the flywheel magneto (mounted on the left-hand side). Carburettor air is drawn from an aperture at the rear of the body along the main-frame tube and thence via trunking through an air filter and smoother to the carburettor.

The clutch is mounted on the right-hand side of the crankcase and just outboard of this is the pre-stretched Duplex chain drive enclosed within the crankcase cover. Gear change is by the left-hand handlebar twist-grip, gear positions and neutral being noted by indentations. Handlebar controls are conventional. the centrally-mounted switch providing five

THROTTLE &   SWITCH   GEARCHANGE & CLUTCH
FRONT BRAKE

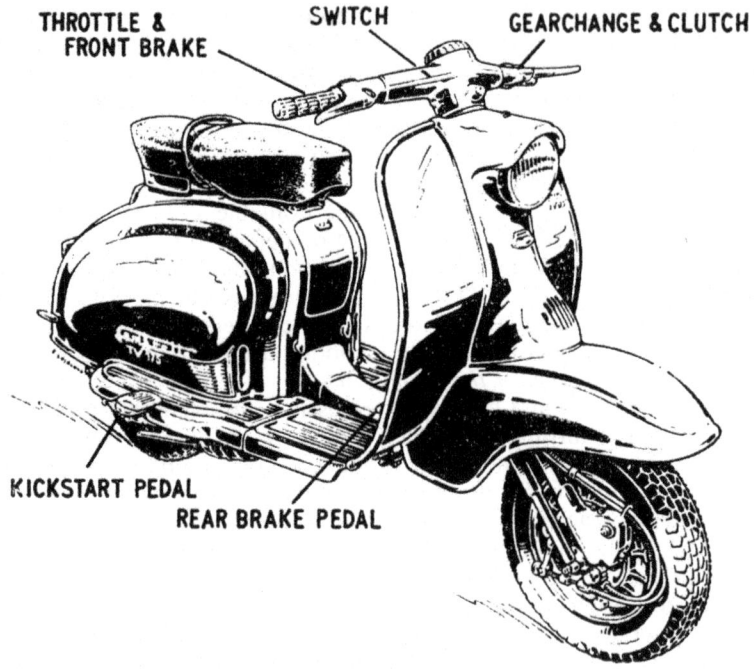

KICKSTART PEDAL
REAR BRAKE PEDAL

FIG. 2. SERIES I TV 175, SHOWING GENERAL ARRANGEMENT
OF CONTROLS

switching positions for lights and ignition whilst the dipper and horn button is mounted near the throttle twist-grip.

The flywheel magneto provides low-tension current to the separate ignition coil (*see* Chapter 10) and 6-volt lighting-current generation with 27 watts output direct to the headlamp and tail lamp, or rectified D.C. for battery charging for parking lights. The battery is of 6·7 ampere-hour capacity.

Standard equipment comprises a dual seat hinged at the front to lift to expose a trap-door over the fuel-tank filler; a small luggage locker; tool kit; speedometer; central stand; and steering-head lock. Numerous extras are available from authorized dealers. Fuel-tank capacity is 1·75 gal, which includes 1·5 pints reserve with nominal fuel consumption 94 m.p.g. Running in traffic with numerous gear changes, etc., fuel consumption is in the region of 80 m.p.g. Top speed is slightly in excess of 60 m.p.h. Essentially the Tv 175 is designed and styled as a luxury-type scooter incorporating the maximum practical size of engine and performance for this class of vehicle.

The Li 150 and Li 125, Series I models closely resemble the Series I Tv 175 in layout and general design and were, in fact, based on the larger model. Although retaining a similar form of engine construction and

FIG. 3. VIEW OF LEFT-HAND SIDE OF SERIES I TV 175,
SIDE PANEL REMOVED

1. Tool locker	3. Carburettor air filter	5. High-tension coil
2. Fuel tank	4. Rectifier	6. Flywheel magneto

layout, however, they differ in detail to the extent that no Tv engine components are used. Basically the same engine is used in both the Li 150 and Li 125 except that, in the smaller size, the bore is reduced from 57 mm to 52 mm to reduce the swept volume from 148 c.c. to 123 c.c. whilst retaining the same compression ratio. Maximum output of the 148 c.c. engine is 6·5 h.p. at 5,300 r.p.m.; and that of the 123 c.c. engine, 5·2 h.p. at 5,200 r.p.m.

The engine group is also somewhat differently arranged, compared with the Tv model (compare Figs. 24 and 29). On the Li models, the clutch is fitted at the wheel end and there is one less gear set in the transmission. The kick-starter is also differently arranged, with the pedal arm cranked to come in a different position. Another difference is that the Duplex chain now runs in an anti-clockwise direction instead of clockwise. Accessibility of clutch and gearbox is, if anything, even easier than on the larger model.

Superficially the main difference in appearance between the Li models and the Tv 175 is the twin-seat arrangement. Externally about the only noticeable difference between the Li 150 and Li 125 is that the former has chrome trim on the side-panels, a key-operated steering lock and rubber strips on the floor (the Li 125 has aluminium strips and painted handlebars),

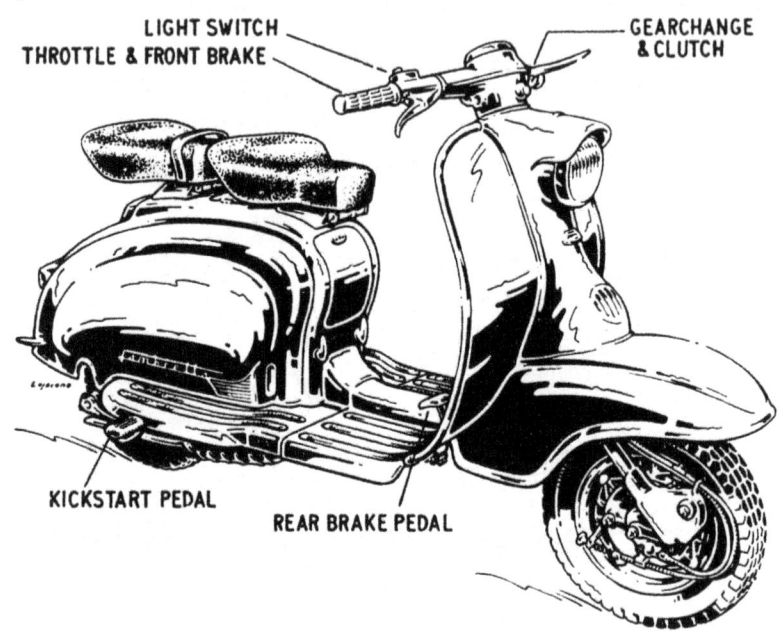

FIG. 4. SERIES I LI MODELS 125 AND 150. BOTH SIMILAR, EXCEPT
FOR DETAIL AND FINISH
Note: separate saddles

although the difference in colour scheme is usually a more positive identification.

Wheels and suspension are the same on the Li models as on the Tv, except that there is no shock absorber on the front suspension (and there are detail differences in the rear shock absorber). Handlebars and controls are essentially similar (but again with detail differences). Electrical equipment on the Li 150 comprises a flywheel magneto and 6-volt 6·7 ampere-hour battery with the flywheel generator feeding the headlamps, rear lamp, speedometer bulb and horn. The battery feeds the parking light and is charged by the flywheel magneto via a rectifier and voltage regulator. The Li 125 has no battery and the flywheel generator feeds the headlamps, rear lamp, pilot lights and horn.

Both Li models have a four-speed gearbox, although the ratios are different. The four gears on the axle and the gear cluster can, however, be interchanged as a group between the two models so that the lower gear ratios of the Li 125 can be fitted to the Li 150 for sidecar use.

Tank capacity on both Li models is 1·9 gal. which includes approximately 1·75 pints reserve, fuel consumption being in the region of 120 m.p.g.

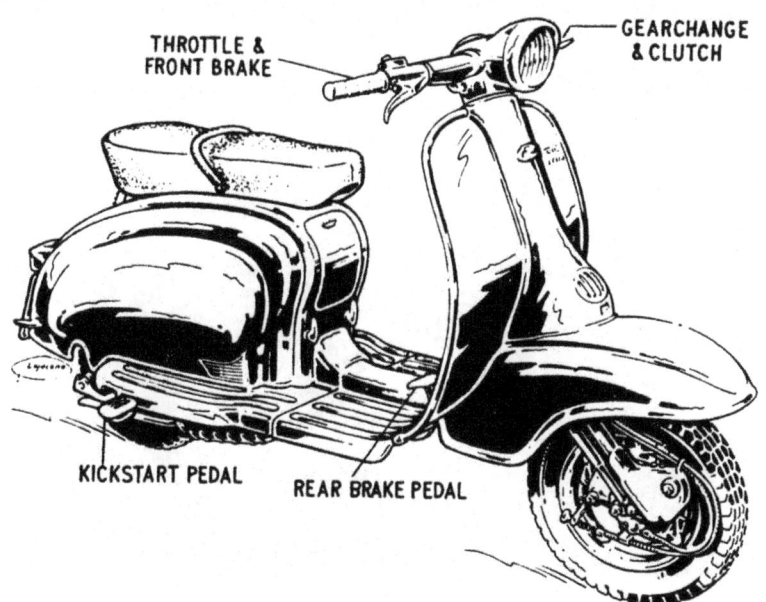

FIG. 5. SERIES II MODELS ARE BASICALLY SIMILAR THROUGHOUT
MAIN CHANGE IS IN MODIFIED HEADLAMP POSITION
Tv 175 Series II (shown) has engine and transmission virtually
identical with the Li models (except for larger bore and stroke).

The original Tv 175 gave way to the Tv 175 Series II in May, 1959, the main external difference being that the headlamp is brought up on to the front of the handlebars and faired in as a unit movable with the handlebars (*see* Fig. 5). Internally the main drive is modified to be the same as employed on the Li models, i.e. the clutch is removed to the rear-axle end and one gear set eliminated, with the simpler servicing facilities offered. The engine unit in the Tv 175 Series II becomes essentially the same as that of the Li series and the bottom end is virtually identical with parts common throughout (but larger piston and cylinder and different connecting rod on the 175 engine).

Later in the same year an identical modification of styling was adopted for the Li models, which became the Li 125 Series II and Li 150 Series II, introduced in October 1959. A number of minor detail modifications have been incorporated and also some more recent changes, but basically both the original and Series II Li machines remain essentially similar. The Series II Li models incorporate a common handlebar design with centrally-mounted ignition cut-out button and steering lock (key operated) underneath.

Electrical equipment on the Li 150 comprises a flywheel magneto and 6-volt, 6·7 ampere-hour battery (4 ampere-hour on earlier models, *see* Chapter 9) with the flywheel generator feeding the headlamps, rear light,

FIG. 6. VIEW OF LEFT-HAND SIDE OF SERIES II MODELS,
SIDE PANEL REMOVED

1. Tool locker	3. Fuel tank	5. Rectifier fuse box
2. Air filter box	4. Carburettor	6. Flywheel magneto

speedometer bulb and horn. The battery is used for the parking lights, and for operating the stop lights (where fitted). The battery is charged by the flywheel generator via a rectifier and voltage regulator (*see* Chapter 9 for details and differences on earlier models). The Li 125 models have no battery and the flywheel generator feeds all the electrical circuit, e.g. headlamps, tail light, horn, speedometer bulb and pilot light.

Wheels and suspension are the same on all models (Li series and Tv series), except that there is no shock absorber on the front suspension on Li models and there are detail differences in the original Li series rear shock absorber. Electrical equipment on the Tv 175 comprises a 6-volt flywheel magneto-generator with a slightly larger battery than on the Li 150. The main difference is that, whilst the main lighting services are fed direct from the generator, the horn is operated on the battery circuit (i.e. it is a D.C.

horn and not A.C. as on the other models) together with the parking lights and stop lights (standard on all Tv models).

All Series II models have a four-speed gearbox although the gear ratios are different. The four gears on the axle and the gear cluster can, however, be interchanged as a group between all three models so that the lower gear ratios of the Li 125 can be fitted to the Li 150 model or the Tv 175 (Series II) for sidecar work.

Tank capacity is the same on all models, with a total volume of 1·9 gal. which includes 1·5 pint approximately reserve supply controlled by a

FIG. 7. SERIES II TV 175 SHOWING COMPONENT DISPOSITION
WITH RECTIFIER-FUSE-RELAY BOX IMMEDIATELY ABOVE REAR WHEEL

switch on the front of the body fairing. Fuel consumption is in the region of 120 m.p.g. in the case of the Li models running at 25–30 m.p.h., reducing to about 70–80 m.p.g. when driven hard. Maximum speed of the Li 125 is approximately 40–45 m.p.h., and of the Li 150, 50–55 m.p.h. Fuel consumption the of Tv 175 is only slightly higher and maximum speed is in the region of 60–65 m.p.h.

Detail differences between the Tv 175 Series II and the original Tv 175 are concerned mainly with standardizing components throughout the whole range of Series II models (125 c.c., 150 c.c. and 175 c.c.), thus rationalizing the spares and maintenance side. Parts throughout the Series II machines are, therefore, largely interchangeable or common, except where specifically noted otherwise. In all cases, however, it is essential to quote the engine and frame numbers in ordering replacement parts. These are to be found on the upper side of the crankcase on the right-hand side immediately in front of the rear shock absorber (engine number) and on the frame tube on the right-hand side just under the tank (frame number).

A further change on Lambretta models was introduced in 1962 with a complete redesign of the fairings and headlamp group to produce the "Slimstyle." These are designated the Series III models of the Li 125, Li 150 and Tv 175, although normally referred to as the 125 Slimstyle, 150 Slimstyle and 175 Slimstyle. These models were first introduced into this country in the latter part of 1962.

Whilst the Series III models retain the same basic engine group and

FIG. 8. SERIES II LI COMPONENT DISPOSITION ESSENTIALLY SIMILAR TO SERIES II TV (COMPARE WITH FIG. 7)

general engineering features, other detail modifications and improvements have also been incorporated. Chief changes include a new carburettor; a new six-pole magneto generator; and a raising of the compression ratio of the engine to give a slight increase in performance. The Series III 175 is also fitted with a disc front brake instead of the normal internal expanding type and is, incidentally, the first two-wheeled production vehicle to be fitted with this type of brake as standard equipment.

Other modifications include a slight change in the shape of the rear transmission casing, a modification of the rear suspension unit, the fitting of a thicker speedometer drive cable, and modification of the wiring circuits so that wiring now terminates on the panel carrying the headlamp bulb rather than on a separate block in the headlamp assembly. In all other respects, however, the Series III models can be considered identical to the earlier models as regards handling and general servicing, etc. Where detail differences occur, these are noted in the text.

A further model was introduced in late 1963 with a larger (198 c.c.) engine but otherwise essentially similar to the Series III 175, and again employing a front wheel disc brake as standard. This model is designated the GT 200 and with the 10·75 b.h.p. engine fitted has a top speed approaching 70 m.p.h. Again the general operating and maintenance instructions apply, except where specific differences are noted in the text.

Another model was introduced in late 1963, designed specifically for the British market, with a larger (198 c.c.) engine, but otherwise essentially similar to the Series III 175, and again employing a front disc brake as standard. This model was originally designated the TV 200, but became known as the GT 200, and with the 10·75 b.h.p. engine fitted has a top speed approaching 70 m.p.h. Again the general operating and main-tenance instructions apply, except where specific differences are noted in the text. The Series III 175 model was subsequently withdrawn from the British market, although it continued to be manufactured and sold in other countries until 1966.

The Li 150 Special was announced as a new model in February 1964. This has similar bodywork to the GT 200, but has a smaller capacity engine and the front brake reverts to the drum type. It offered considerable improvement in performance over the earlier 150 models because of internal engine changes.

The J range were also announced in 1964 and were basically completely new designs, both in construction and appearance. These were much lighter models, with the frame of pressed steel incorporating integral leg-shields, an upright cylinder, different engine mounting and a three-speed gearbox. Two models were produced initially, with 50 c.c. and 100 c.c. engines, respectively, but only the latter appeared in this country where it became known as the Cento. It was followed in 1965 by a larger version, the J 125. This retained the three-speed gearbox, but the engine had a modified crankshaft to accommodate the higher power, and im-proved engine mounting. Both these modifications were later incorporated in the Cento.

A new version of the Li series appeared in 1966, known as the SX 200. This was intended to replace the GT 200 on the British market (and the Tv 175 elsewhere). The only external difference between the SX 200 and the GT 200 was a slight modification of the side panels, which incorporated an arrow-shaped motif on the later model. Internally, however, there were numerous detail design changes in the engine, aimed particularly at giving a smoother and quieter performance.

Concurrent with the SX 200, a new J series model appeared to replace the Cento and J 125. This was known as the J 125 Starstream and incor-porated a number of changes. Whilst retaining the pressed steel construc-tion the frame shapes were altered to provide more of a Lambretta "family likeness." Another external difference was the bigger headlamp fitted. Internally the engine was slightly modified in detail, with new mounts, and, most significant of all, a four-speed gearbox. It was further modified again in 1967 by slight changes to the bodywork shape and mudguards, this particular version being known as the J125 Super Starstream. Relatively few of these models were sold in Britain, however. Both Starstream models, in fact, had a limited production run and were eventually phased out in favour of the Luna line with 50 c.c. and 75 c.c. engines. Only the latter were imported, in two models known as the Vega and Comet and are more properly classed as mopeds rather than scooters. Because they are quite different small models, no specific details are given in this handbook (although the engines were based on the J range). They are mentioned mainly to show their place in the evolution of the Lambretta line.

Rationalization of scooter production continued in March 1967 with the introduction of the SX 150, which replaced all previous 125 and 150 models in the Li series. Outwardly it was essentially similar to the Li 150 Special, but with a considerably improved power output, small detail changes internally, and a superior performance due, in no small part, to the altered gear ratios.

This model had a run of two years in production but was replaced in 1969 by two new models in the Li Series—the Grand Prix 150 and Grand Prix 200. Externally these models are distinguished by rectangular headlamps and the use of bold colours for the bodywork, together with matt black finish for small parts. Internally detail differences are so numerous as to make them virtually new models, the main changes being engine modifications to increase both the power and the rev. range, with altered gear ratios to suit, and modifications to the clutch design to take the increased power.

The latest model to appear (in 1970) is the Li Series 125 DL, which is virtually a smaller version of the two Grand Prix models, making three Li Series models in all in current production (1970).

SUMMARY OF LAMBRETTA MODELS

DATE	MODEL	REMARKS
	A and B	123 c.c. engine on central-girder frame.
1952	C	Single-tube frame with independently sprung rear wheel.
1955 (in Britain)	D and LD	Pivotally mounted engine-transmission unit with torsion bar rear suspension. Two engine sizes available: 125 c.c. and 150 c.c.

Date	Model	Remarks
1957	125 LD Mark III	D model with engine covers and added fairings.
1958	125 LD Mark IV	
1958	Tv 175	Horizontal engine with forward facing cylinder. Very few imported into Britain.
1959	Li 125 Series I Li 150 Series I	Wheel diameter increased to 10 inches. Twin seat arrangement. Duplex chain drive. Four-speed gearboxes.
1959–60	Tv 175 Series II	Similar to Li models, but with shock absorbers behind front forks.
1959–60	Li 125 Series II Li 150 Series II	Modified styling (similar to TV 175 Series II). Four-speed gearboxes.
1962	Li 125 Series III (125 Slimstyle) Li 150 Series III (150 Slimstyle) Tv 175 Series III (175 Slimstyle)	Improved styling: same engine group but with detail changes giving improved performance. 175 model fitted with disc front brake.
1963	Tv 200 (later known as GT 200)	More powerful model replacing the Tv 175 Series III.
1964	Li 150 Special	Similar bodywork to Tv 200; detail engine changes giving improved performance over Li 150 Series III. Drum front brake.
1964	J Range 50 c.c.	None in Britain.
	J Range 100 c.c. (Cento)	Very few in Britain.
	J 125	Pressed steel frame with integral legshields; light construction; upright cylinder; three-speed gearbox.
1966	SX 200	Replacement for the GT 200; many detail engine group modifications; improved performance.
1966	J 125 Starstream	Modified styling, bigger headlamps; some engine changes; four-speed gearbox. Replacement for the Cento and L 125.

DATE	MODEL	REMARKS
1967	J 125 Super Starstream	Minor changes to bodywork and mudguards.
1967	SX 150	Replacement for Li 125 and 150 Series III models.
1968	Luna Line (50 c.c.)*	Moped.
	Luna Line (75 c.c.)*	Two models — Vega and Cometa.
1969	Grand Prix 150 (GP 150)*	Extensive engine group modi-
	Grand Prix 200 (GP 200)*	fications; improved styling; rectangular headlamps. Continuation of the Li Series.
1970	125 DL*	Smaller engined version of the GP models.

* Current productions (1970).

SPECIFICATIONS
Lambretta Li 125

Overall length. 71¾ in.
Overall width (*over handlebars*). 28 in.
Maximum height. 40¾ in.
Ground clearance. 6½ in.
Wheelbase. 51 in.
Weight (*unladen*). 230 lb.
Engine. Single cylinder two-stroke, air-cooled; bore 52 mm; stroke 58 mm capacity 123 c.c.; compression ratio 7·0:1; peak power 5·2 b.h.p. at 5,200 r.p.m.
Ignition. Four-pole flywheel magneto with external high-tension coil; 14 mm long-reach spark plug, British equivalent, Champion N5 or N84, spark-timing 22–24 degrees before T.D.C.
Transmission (*primary*). Duplex chain with two shock absorbers (one on sprocket and one on pinion).
Gearbox. Four-speed,
    gear ratios (wheel r.p.m.: crankshaft r.p.m.)—
    1st, 1:17·40; 2nd, 1:10·71; 3rd, 1:7·47; 4th, 1:5·65.
Clutch. Multi-disc type in oil bath.
Carburettor. Dell'Orto MB 18 BS 5.
Wheels. Pressed-steel, split rims (wheels interchangeable front and rear), tyre size 10 in × 3½ in.
Maximum speed. 42–45 m.p.h.

Lambretta Li 150

Overall length. 71¾ in.
Overall width (*over handlebars*). 28 in.

Maximum height. 40¾ in.
Ground clearance. 6½ in.
Wheelbase. 51 in.
Weight (unladen). 231 lb.
Engine. Single cylinder, two-stroke, air-cooled; bore 57 mm; stroke 58 mm; capacity 148 c.c.; compression ratio 7·0:1; peak power 6·5 b.h.p. at 5,300 r.p.m. four-pole.
Ignition. Four-pole flywheel magneto with external high-tension coil; 14 mm long-reach spark plug, British equivalent, Champion N5 or N84, spark-timing 22–24 degrees before T.D.C.
Transmission (primary). Duplex chain with two shock absorbers (one on sprocket and one on pinion).
Gearbox. Four-speed,
   gear ratios (wheel r.p.m.:   crankshaft r.p.m.)—
   1st, 1:13·95; 2nd, 1:9·00; 3rd, 1:6·7;   4th, 1:5·22.
Clutch. Multi-disc type in oil bath.
Carburettor. Dell'Orto MB 19 BS 5.
Wheels. Pressed-steel, split rims (wheels interchangeable front and rear), tyre size 10 in. × 3½ in.
Maximum speed. 50–55 m.p.h.

Lambretta Tv 175

Overall length. 71¾ in.
Overall width (over handlebars). 28 in.
Maximum height. 42 in.
Ground clearance. 6½ in.
Wheelbase. 51 in.
Weight (unladen). 264 lb (original model).
                    242 lb (Series II).
Engine. Single cylinder two-stroke air-cooled.

Series I	Series II
Bore 60 mm;	Bore 62 mm;
Stroke 60 mm;	Stroke 58 mm;
Capacity 170 c.c.;	Capacity 175 c.c.;
Compression ratio 7·5:1;	Compression ratio 7·6:1;
Peak power 8·6 b.h.p. at 6,000 r.p.m.	Peak power 8·6 b.h.p. at 6,000 r.p.m.

Ignition. Four-pole flywheel magneto with external ignition coil; 14 mm long-reach spark plug, British equivalent, Champion N5 or N48, spark-timing 26–28 degrees before T.D.C. (Series I); 23 degrees (Series II).
Transmission (primary). Duplex chain with torque limiter.

Gearbox. Four speed,
  Gear ratios (wheel r.p.m.: crankshaft r.p.m.)—
    Series I: 1st, 1 : 14·32; 2nd, 1 : 9·77; 3rd, 1 : 7·30; 4th, 1 : 5·69.
    Series II: 1st, 1 : 12·5; 2nd, 1 : 8·76; 3rd, 1 : 6·30; 4th, 1 : 4·82.
Clutch. Multi-disc type in oil bath.
Carburettor. Dell'Orto MB 23 BS 5 (Series I and II).
                MB 21 BS 5 (Series II, later models).
Wheels. Pressed steel, split rims (wheels interchangeable front and rear)
  tyre size 10 in. × 3½ in.
Maximum speed. 64 m.p.h.

Lambretta GT 200

Overall length. 71 in.
Overall width. 27½ in.
Maximum height. 40½ in.
Ground clearance. 6½ in.
Wheel base. 51 in.
Weight (unladen). 242 lb.
Engine. Single cylinder two-stroke, forced-air-cooled; bore 66 mm;
  stroke 58 mm; capacity 198 c.c.; compression ratio 8:1; peak power
  10·75 b.h.p. at 5,700 r.p.m.
Ignition. Six-pole 60-watt flywheel magneto with external high tension
  coil. Spark plug: during running period—heat range 225 (Bosch
  scale); after running-in period—heat range 226 or 240 according to
  conditions of use.
Battery. Six-volt eight ampere-hour capacity.
Transmission. Double row chain with two shock dampers.
Gearbox. Four-speed constant mesh in oil bath.
  Gear ratios—
  1st, 1:11·086; 2nd, 1:7·974; 3rd, 1:5·810; 4th, 1:4·462.
Clutch. Multi-disc in oil bath.
Carburettor. Dell'Orto SH 20 automatic with central float chamber;
  no needle. Air filter cartridge type incorporated in air intake box.
Fuel tank. Capacity 1·9 gallons.
Wheels and brakes. Pressed-steel, split rims (wheels interchangeable
  front and rear), tyre size 10 in. × 3½ in. Brakes: front—disc brake;
  rear—internal expanding.
Central frame. In steel tube. Centre stand with two arms.
Bodywork. In pressed steel sheet.
Front suspension. Trailing links, carrying variable pitch helical springs
  and shock absorbers.
Rear suspension. Swinging engine unit with shock absorber carrying one
  helical spring of variable pitch.

Lambretta SX 200

Overall weights and dimensions. As GT 200.

Engine. Single-cylinder two-stroke, forced-air-cooled; bore 66 mm; stroke 58 mm; capacity 198 c.c.; compression ratio 7:1; peak power 10·35 b.h.p. at 5,500 r.p.m.

Ignition. As GT 200 (Ducati 6-volt flywheel magneto).

Battery. As GT 200.

Gearbox. Four-speed constant mesh in oil bath.

   Gear ratios—
   1st, 1:12·522; 2nd, 1:8·762; 3rd, 1:6·304; 4th, 1:4·819.

Carburettor. Dell'Orto SH 20 (same as GT 200 except for main jet size).

Wheels, brakes and other details. As GT 200.

Lambretta Tv 175 Series III (Slimstyle)

Overall length. 71 in.

Overall width. 27½ in.

Maximum height. 41 in.

Ground clearance. 6½ in.

Wheelbase. 51 in.

Weight (unladen). 242 lb.

Engine. Single cylinder two-stroke, forced-air-cooled; bore 62 mm; stroke 58 mm; capacity 175 c.c.; compression ratio 8:1; peak power 8·75 b.h.p. at 5,300 r.p.m.

Ignition. Six-pole 27 watt flywheel magneto with external high tension coil. Spark plug: during running-in period—heat range 225 (Bosch scale); after running-in period—heat range 226 or 240 according to conditions of use.

Battery. Six-volt eight ampere-hour capacity.

Transmission. Double row chain with two shock dampers.

Gearbox. Four-speed constant mesh in oil bath.

   Gear ratios—
   1st, 1:12·522; 2nd, 1:8·762; 3rd, 1:6·304; 4th, 1:4·819.

Clutch. Multi-disc in oil bath.

Carburettor. Dell'Orto SH 20 automatic, with central float chamber; no needle. Air filter cartridge type incorporated in air intake box.

Fuel tank. Capacity 1·9 gallons.

Wheels and brakes. Pressed-steel, split rims (wheels interchangeable front and rear), tyre size 10 in. × 3½ in. Brakes: front—disc brake; rear—internal expanding.

Central frame. In steel tube. Centre stand with two arms.

Bodywork. In pressed steel sheet.

Front suspension. Trailing links, carrying variable pitch helical springs and shock absorbers.

Rear suspension. Swinging engine unit with shock absorber carrying one helical spring of variable pitch.

Lambretta Li 150 Series III (Slimstyle)

Overall length. 71 in.
Overall width. 27½ in.
Maximum height. 41 in.
Ground clearance. 6½ in.
Wheelbase. 51 in.
Weight (unladen). 231 lb.
Engine. Single cylinder two-stroke, forced-air-cooled; bore 57 mm; stroke 58 mm; capacity 148 c.c.; compression ratio 7·5:1; peak power 6·6 b.h.p. at 5,300 r.p.m.
Ignition. Six-pole 27 watt flywheel magneto with external high tension coil; spark plug 225 heat range (Bosch scale); long reach. Fixed ignition.
Battery (where fitted). Six-volt eight ampere-hour capacity.
Transmission. Double row chain.
Gearbox. Four-speed constant mesh in oil bath.
  Gear ratios—
  1st, 1:13·95; 2nd, 1:9·00; 3rd, 1:6·67; 4th, 1:5·22.
Clutch. Multi-disc in oil bath.
Carburettor. Dell'Orto SH 19 automatic, with central float chamber; no needle. Silencing air filter.
Fuel tank. Capacity 1·9 gallons.
Wheels and brakes. Pressed-steel, split rims (wheels interchangeable front and rear), tyre size 10 in. × 3½ in. Internal expansion brakes.
Central frame. In steel tube. Centre stand with two arms.
Bodywork. In pressed steel sheet.
Front suspension. Trailing links, variable pitch helical springs.
Rear suspension. Swinging engine unit with shock absorber carrying a helical spring or varying pitch.

Lambretta Li 125 Series III (Slimstyle)

Overall length. 71 in.
Overall width. 27½ in.
Maximum height. 41 in.
Ground clearance. 6½ in.
Wheelbase. 51 in.
Weight (unladen). 230 lb.
Engine. Single cylinder two-stroke, forced-air-cooled; bore 52 mm; stroke 58 mm; capacity 123 c.c.; compression ratio 7·5:1; peak power 5·5 b.h.p. at 5,200 r.p.m.

Ignition. Six-pole 27 watt flywheel magneto with external high tension coil; spark plug 225 heat range (Bosch scale); long reach. Fixed ignition.

Battery (*where fitted*). Six-volt eight ampere-hour capacity.

Transmission. Chain in oil bath.

Gearbox. Four-speed constant mesh in oil bath.

Gear ratios—

1st, 1:17·40; 2nd, 1:10·71; 3rd, 1:7·47; 4th, 1:5·65.

Clutch. Multi-disc in oil bath.

Carburettor. Dell'Orto SH 19 automatic, with central float chamber; no needle.

Fuel tank. Capacity 1·9 gallons.

Wheels and brakes. Pressed-steel, split rims (wheels interchangeable front and rear), tyre size 10 in. × 3½ in. Internal expansion brakes.

Central frame. In steel tube. Centre stand with two arms.

Bodywork. In pressed steel sheet.

Front suspension. Trailing links, variable pitch helical springs.

Rear suspension. Swinging engine unit with shock absorber carrying two helical springs of different pitch.

Lambretta SX 150

Overall length. 71 in.

Overall width. 27½ in.

Overall height. 40 in.

Wheelbase. 51 in.

Weight (*unladen*). 265 lb.

Engine. Single-cylinder two-stroke, forced-air-cooled; bore 57 mm; stroke 58 mm; capacity 148 c.c.; compression ratio 7:1; peak power 9·38 h.p. at 5,600 r.p.m.

Carburettor. Dell'Orto SH 1/20 with central float chamber; no needle.

Ignition. By flywheel magneto and external high-tension coil. Spark plug 225 heat range (Bosch scale). Long reach. Fixed ignition advance.

Clutch. Multi-disc in oilbath.

Transmission. Double row chain.

Gear box. Four-speed constant mesh in oil bath. Rear wheel/driving shaft r.p.m. ratio—

1st, 0·0652; 2nd, 0·0932; 3rd, 0·1254; 4th, 0·1770.

Wheels and brakes. Interchangeable wheels. Rims: in pressed sheet, split in two halves. Brakes: internal expansion.

Tyres: 3·50 × 10 in.

Tyre pressures—

Front: 12·8 lb/sq in.

Rear (driver only): 18 lb/sq in.

Rear (with pillion): 32 lb/sq in.

CONDENSED SPECIFICATIONS OF ALL LAMBRETTA MODELS

	125 Li I	150 Li I	175 TV2	125 Li II	150 Li II	175 TV3	125 Li III	150 Li III	200 TV
Weight kg	104	104	107	104	104	110	104	104	110
Length mm	1825	1825	1825	1825	1825	1800	1800	1800	1800
Height mm	1038	1038	1060	1060	1060	1035	1035	1035	1035
Width mm	710	710	710	710	710	700	700	700	700
Capacity c.c.	123	148	175	123	148	175	123	148	198
Bore mm	52	57	62	52	57	62	52	57	66
Stroke mm	58	58	58	58	58	58	58	58	58
Max output b.h.p.	5·2	6·5	8·6	5·2	6·5	8·7	5·5	6·6	10·7
Max output r.p.m.	5200	5300	6000	5200	5300	5300	5200	5300	5700
Compression ratio	7·0	7·0	7·6	7·0	7·0	8·0	7·0	7·0	8·0
Petrol/oil ratio "₀	4	4	4	4/2	4/2	4	2	2	4
Max speed m.p.h.	47	53	60	47	54	64	49	55	66
Gearbox speeds	4	4	4	4	4	4	4	4	4
Tyre size × 10 in.	3·50	3·50	3·50	3·50	3·50	3·50	3·50	3·50	3·50
Tyre pressures front. lb/sq in. rear	18 28	18 28	18 28	18 28	18 28	18 28	18 28	18 28	18 28
Fuel tank capacity gal	1·7	1·9	1·9	1·9	1·9	1·9	1·9	1·9	1·9
Gearbox capacity pt.	1·2	1·2	1·2	1·2	1·2	1·0	1·0	1·0	1·0
Ignition timing ° BTDC	23	23	23	23	23	23	23	23	23
Carb. choke size mm	18	19	23/21	18	19	20	18	18	20

CONDENSED SPECIFICATIONS OF ALL LAMBRETTA MODELS

	150 Li S	200 SX	150 SX	150 GP	200 GP	125 DL	100 Cento	125 J	125 Star	75 Vega
Weight kg	109	110	104	120	123	118	88	88	90	76
Length mm	1800	1800	1800	1800	1800	1800	1690	1690	1690	1690
Height mm	1035	1035	1035	1012	1012	1012	1030	1030	1030	1028
Width mm	700	700	700	680	680	680	630	630	630	660
Capacity c.c.	148	198	148	148	198	123	98	122	122	75
Bore mm	57	66	57	57	66	52	51	57	57	46·4
Stroke mm	58	58	58	58	58	58	58	48	48	44
Max output b.h.p.	7·6	10·3	8·7	8·7	11·7	7·3	4·7	5·8	5·8	5·2
Max output r.p.m.	5600	5500	5600	6300	6200	6200	5300	5300	5300	6000
Compression ratio	7·5	7·3	7·0	7·8	7·3	7·8	7·5	7·4	7·4	9·3
Petrol/oil ratio %	2	4	2	2	4	2	2	2	2	2
Max speed m.p.h.	58	65	61	62	69	57	47	54	54	52
Gearbox speeds	4	4	4	4	4	4	3	3	4	4
Tyre size × 10 in.	3·50	3·50	3·50	3·50	3·50	3·50	3·00	3·00	3·00	3·00
Tyre pressures front	18	18	18	18	18	18	18	18	18	22
lb/sq in. rear	28	28	28	28	28	28	28	28	28	26
Fuel tank capacity gal	1·9	1·9	1·9	1·9	1·9	1·9	1·3	1·3	1·3	1·3
Gearbox capacity pt.	1·0	1·0	1·0	1·0	1·0	1·0	0·7	0·7	0·9	0·9
Ignition timing ° BTDC	23	23	23	21	21	21	24	24	24	21
Carb. choke size mm	18	20	20	22	22	20	16	16	16	20

Lambretta J 125

Overall length. 66½ in.

Overall width. 24¾ in.

Maximum height. 40¼ in.

Wheelbase. 47 in.

Weight (unladen). 198 lb.

Engine. Single-cylinder two-stroke, forced-air-cooled; bore 57 mm; stroke 48 mm; capacity 122·5 c.c.; compression ratio 7·45:1; peak power 5·8 h.p. at 5,300 r.p.m.

Carburettor. Dell'Orto SHB 16/18, with central float chamber; no tapered needle. Air filter: cartridge type incorporated in air intake box.

Ignition. By flywheel magneto and external H.T. coil—spark plug 240 heat range (Bosch scale) long screw thread: 18 mm. Fixed ignition advanced.

Clutch. Multi-disc in oil bath.

Gear box. Four-speed constant mesh gear box. Alternatively keyed with the rear axle.

Rear wheel/driving shaft r.p.m. ratio—

1st speed, 0·0713; 2nd speed, 0·0989; 3rd speed, 0·1345; 4th speed, 0·1739.

Wheels and brakes. Interchangeable wheels. Rims: in pressed sheet, split in two halves. Brakes: mechanical with internal expansion.

Tyres: 3 × 10 in.

Tyre pressures—

Front 18·5 lb sq in. (driver only).

20   lb sq in. (driver and passenger).

Rear 28·5 lb sq in. (driver only).

35·5 lb sq in. (driver and passenger).

2 Handling the Lambretta

THE Li and Tv Lambrettas represent a noticeable improvement in performance over the earlier model Lambrettas, particularly in the matter of engine flexibility. The engine itself has a wider spread of power which, together with the four-speed gearbox, gives strong low-speed pulling power at one end and lively top-gear performance at the other. Flexibility is emphasized by the fact that there is a marked absence of "snatch" when

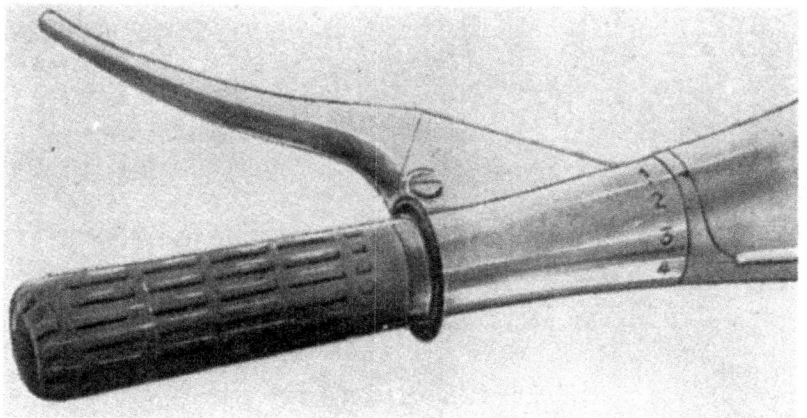

FIG. 9. GEAR-SHIFT IS BY LEFT-HAND TWIST-GRIP CONTROL, WHICH ALSO INCORPORATES CLUTCH-LEVER ASSEMBLY
Gear positions are marked on rotating member

speed is reduced in top gear, in which on the 175 engine one can drop as low as 15 m.p.h. and still pull away smoothly, although this would not be normal practice. The gear shift is there to be used and good driving technique demands that the gear ratios be employed to full advantage by changing gear whenever necessary.

The gear change is identical on all the Li and Tv models, and is accomplished by rotary movement of the left-hand twist grip on the handlebars (*see* Fig. 9). Gear positions are clearly marked on the housing, the first change from neutral to first gear position (1) being accomplished by rotating the grip in a backward direction, and all subsequent changes to higher gears by rotary movement in the forward direction, In changing down, of course, the action is reversed. Gear engagement is smooth and positive, with a total rotary movement of the twist grip of about 100°. All changes are quiet except that in changing from neutral to first gear a certain amount of "clunk" is usually inevitable, even with correct clutch adjustment and movement. The clutch action itself is smooth and calls for no particular skill to master. Typical speeds in gears are summarized in Table 1.

The various control positions are illustrated in Figs. 9, 10 and 11, these being the same on all models apart from the switches (*see* Chapters 9 and

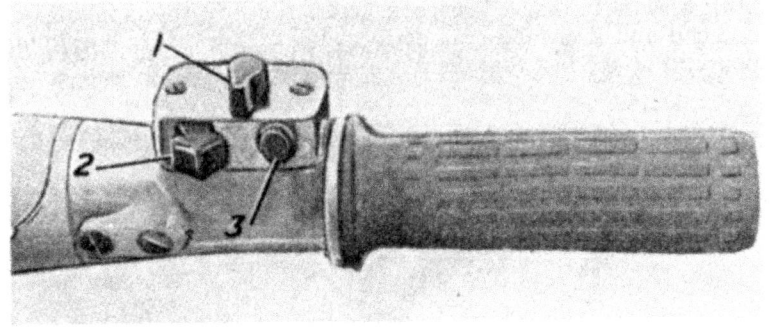

FIG. 10. LIGHTING AND HANDLEBAR SWITCHES DIFFER ON
TV AND LI MODELS

Handlebar switch for Li models as shown: 1, light switch; 2, dip-switch; 3, horn button. Press-button cut-out switch at centre of handlebars. Handlebar switch on Tv models incorporates dip-switch and horn button. Central light switch incorporates key-operated ignition.

10). Fuel tap and choke controls are mounted on the lower part of the vertical fairing in front of the saddle (Fig. 11). The right-hand knob controls the choke whilst the left-hand knob is the fuel tap. "Closed" positions of both controls are when the knob is pointing *upwards*. The choke is operated by turning the knob through 180 degrees (i.e. a complete half turn). The fuel tap has three positions. Pointing vertically upwards, the fuel supply from the tank is turned "off." To turn "on," the tap is rotated through 90 degrees to point to the left. The third switching position, which connects the reserve fuel supply in the tank, is engaged by rotating a further 90 degrees so that the point of the knob is vertically downwards. It is recommended that the fuel tap always be turned off when the machine is not in use and to the normal "open" position when driving.

The fuel-tank filler is accessible through the top fairing (*see* Fig. 23). In the case of the Li models a hinged flap between the two saddles must be lifted to expose the filler cap. On the Tv 175 the dual-saddle must first be released, by pulling on a lever at the rear beneath the grille fairing, then hinged forward to expose the hinged flap and filler underneath.

All the new engines are designed expressly to operate on a very economical petrol-oil mixture, the proportion of oil to petrol specified being only 4 per cent (or 1 part in 25). Two- or three-star petrol is quite suitable for all engines, except those with 200 c.c. engines (GT, SX or GP), where maximum performance demands the use of four-star petrol.

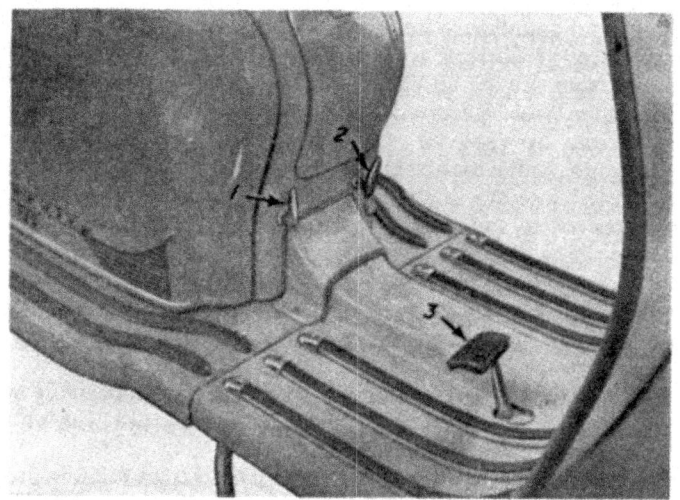

FIG. 11. CHOKE CONTROL (1) ROTATES 180° ANTICLOCKWISE
TO BRING CHOKE INTO OPERATION
Fuel tap (2) has three positions: "off" vertically up, "on" turned at
right angles (to left), and "reserve" in fully down position.

A two-stroke oil is specifically recommended (not normal car engine crankcase oil, which contains additives). This should be SAE 30 or SAE 40 viscosity, mixed in the proportion of 1 part oil to 25 parts of petrol (but *see* also Table 3, page 26). Two-stroke oil from any of the major brands is suitable.

It is most important to understand that although the recommended oil ratio is quite low *it is absolutely imperative that this ratio is maintained.* The use of petrol without added oil will quickly result in serious damage to the engine.

The standard mixture is quite satisfactory for running-in a new engine although it is particularly important for the first 500 to 1,000 miles, to drive carefully, avoid full-throttle running in any gear and avoid heavily-loaded running, e.g. hill-climbing in a high gear. Speed in itself is not necessarily harmful, but no new engine can be expected to give a smooth performance until fully run in. Excessive speeding when the engine is new and relatively stiff can cause overheating and permanent damage. Slow-speed running, with heavy loads on the engine, is particularly bad for the bearings; hence the need for changing down to a lower gear under such circumstances. The life and subsequent performance of the engine depends very much on the treatment it receives during the running-in period, whilst a number of other features also require careful attention during the first 500 miles or so (see Chapter 3). The engine will not be fully run-in and completely free until after some 1,500 to 2,000 miles.

Maintenance of correct tyre pressures is of equal importance for comfortable, safe driving and also to obtain maximum life and minimum trouble from the tyres. Recommended tyre pressures for the various models are summarized in Table 4. It will be noticed that, with a pillion passenger, a substantial increase in rear-tyre pressure is called for, optimum pressure being related to the load carried. In point of fact, recommended tyre pressures are to some extent arbitrary and based largely on giving a comfortable ride with a reasonable degree of distortion and flexing of the tyre. For fast solo riding it may be beneficial to increase the rear-tyre pressure to a figure of about 28 lb per sq in. and the front-tyre pressure to 18 lb per sq in. to improve traction, although this is only obtained at some sacrifice in comfort of ride.

Driving and handling of the new Lambretta models on the road follows conventional scooter practice, which is generally well known and needs no further description here.*

All the new models have enhanced stability and road-holding properties, chiefly as a result of the adoption of the slightly larger wheels. The new engine design and four-speed gearbox offer better acceleration through the gears and braking performance has also been improved. Both brakes are light in action and capable of precise control, although the same consideration applies, as with all two-wheeled vehicles, that braking must be done cautiously on slippery surfaces.

Stopping distance on good, dry surfaces is in the region of 30–35 feet from 30 m.p.h., with brakes in good condition and correctly adjusted. There is a marked dipping action of the front suspension when the front wheel is heavily braked, owing to the trailing position of the wheel. Correct use of the brakes demands that both be used equally, both to give most efficient braking and to equalize wear. The servicing of the brakes is dealt with in Chapter 5.

Starting procedure is similar on all models. It is easiest to kick-start the engine standing on the right of the machine, with the scooter pulled up on to its centre stand. The gear-change twist grip must be set to neutral (0) as the kick-start will not engage otherwise. The fuel tap is then turned to the

---

* The novice may refer to The First Book of the Lambretta, Pitman.

open position (90 degrees to the left) and the choke knob turned anticlockwise through 180 degrees. Little or no throttle opening is required and, when kicked over, the engine should start on the first or second kick. It can then be warmed up by opening the throttle slightly, returning the choke control to its original position as soon as possible. The choke control should always be returned to the "off" position before driving off, varying the warming-up time according to the weather. This is only necessary for starting from cold, and in all other circumstances the engine can be kick-started directly after opening the fuel tap. Excessive use of the choke (e.g. leaving it operating too long) will result in an over-rich mixture being drawn in and a flooded engine.

To stop the engine it is only necessary to close the throttle and press the ignition cut-out button, holding down until the engine dies. Before stopping, neutral gear should normally be engaged.

The engine may be push-started in gear, if this becomes necessary, selecting first gear for this purpose. It is possible also to push-start in second gear satisfactorily, but not in higher gears.

TABLE 1

APPROXIMATE MAXIMUM SPEEDS IN GEARS*

Model	1st gear	2nd gear	3rd gear	4th gear
Li 125 .	14.5 m.p.h.	23 m.p.h.	34 m.p.h.	44 m.p.h.
Li 150 .	18.5 m.p.h.	30 m.p.h.	38 m.p.h.	50 m.p.h.
Tv 175 .	24 m.p.h.	35 m.p.h.	46 m.p.h.	56–8 m.p.h.
GT 200 and 200 SX .	—	—	—	58–60 m.p.h.

* Driver sitting upright.

TABLE 2

EQUIVALENT LUBRICANTS

	Shell	B.P.	Esso	Mobil	Castrol	Duckhams
4% mixture (1:25 ratio)	Shell TT or Shell 2T	Energol two-stroke oil	Esso two-stroke oil	Mobilmix TT		Duckhams two-stroke oil
1 pint per gallon (1:16 ratio)	Shell 2T	Energol SAE 30	Essolube 30	Mobiloil A	Castrol XL Castrol two-stroke oil	NOL Thirty

TABLE 3
PETROIL MIXTURES
(SAE 30 or SAE 40 two-stroke oil)

Model	Oil proportion	
	Self-mixing	Non-self-mixing
Li Series I (125 and 150) . . .	4%	4%
Li Series II (125 and 150), early . .	4%	4%
after 1962	4%	2%
Tv 175 Series II	4%	4%
Tv 175 Series III	4%	4%
Li Series III (Slimstyle)		
Li 125 and 150	4%	2%
GT 200	4%	4%
SX 150	4%	2%
SX 200	4%	4%
150 Special	4%	2%
Grand Prix		
GP 150	4%	2%
GP 200	4%	4%
125 DL	4%	2%

TABLE 4
RECOMMENDED TYRE PRESSURES
(lb/sq in.)

Model	Solo		With pillion passenger	
	Front	Rear	Front	Rear
Li Series I (125 and 150) .	18	28	18	32
Li Series II (125 and 150) .	18	28	18	32
Tv Series II . . .	18	28	18	32
Tv Series III . . .	18	28	18	32
Li Series III (Slimstyle)				
Li 125 and 150 . .	18	28	18	34
GT 200 . .	18	28	18	34
SX 150 . .	18	28	18	34
SX 200 . .	18	28	18	34
150 Special . .	18	28	18	34
Grand Prix				
GP 150 . .	18	28	18	34
GP 200 . .	18	28	18	34
125 DL . .	18	28	18	34
J Series . . .	18	28	18	30
Luna Series . .	22	30	—	—

TABLE 5

GEARBOX LUBRICATION

(SAE 90 oil*—all models)

Model	Capacity	
	Pints	Litres
Li Series I (125 and 150) .	$1\frac{1}{4}$	0·7
Li Series II (125 and 150) .	$1\frac{1}{2}$	0·7
Tv Series I	$2\frac{1}{2}$†	1·4†
Tv Series III . . .	$1\frac{1}{4}$	0·7
Tv Series III . . .	$1\frac{1}{4}$	0·7
Li Series III (Slimstyle)		
Li 125 and Li 150 . .	$1\frac{1}{4}$	0·7
GT 200 . . .	$1\frac{1}{4}$	0·7
SX 150 . . .	$1\frac{1}{4}$	0·7
SX 150 . . .	$1\frac{1}{4}$	0·7
150 Special . . .	$1\frac{1}{4}$	0·7
Grand Prix		
GP 150 . . .	$1\frac{1}{4}$	0·7
GP 200 . . .	$1\frac{1}{4}$	0·7
125 DL . . .	$1\frac{1}{4}$	0·7
J Series (3-speed) . .	$\frac{3}{4}$	0·45
J Series (4-speed) . .	1	0·55

   * E.g. Castrol ST or equivalent. Extreme pressure (EP) oils must *not* be used.

   † SAE 30 oil for this model only.

3 Regular maintenance

ENGINE lubrication is provided by oil mixed with the petrol. The gear-box unit is lubricated by a separate filling of oil which is retained within the crankcase unit and requires periodic topping-up and change of oil, when specified. Oil grade for all models except Tv Series I is SAE 90

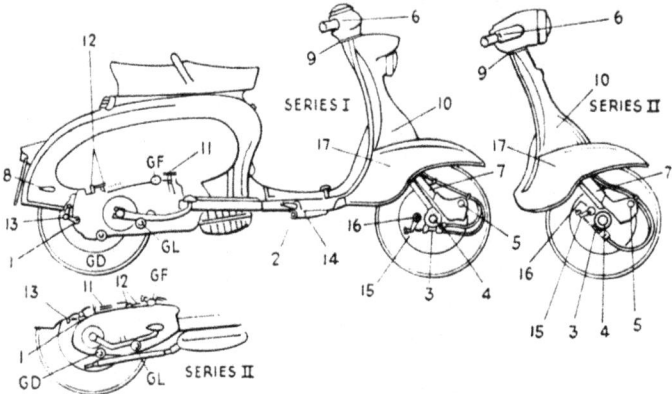

FIG. 12. LUBRICATION POINTS, TV 175 SERIES I AND SERIES II
(*See* table for key.)

but not an E.P. (extreme pressure) oil which normally contains sulphur and could be harmful. The capacity of the crankcase to the level plug is 1¼ pints. The Tv Series I takes 2½ pints of SAE 30.

Other lubrication points requiring periodic attention are either provided with grease nipples, or presented as pivot points, etc., for lubrication with an oilcan. Parts such as the side-panel catches, hand-lever pivots, stand pivots, steering-head bearings and twist-grip bearings are greased on assembly and do not normally need regreasing, except when obviously needing some attention.

Lubrication points are basically similar on all models, the lubrication diagrams of Figs. 12–14 providing a complete guide. Only one oil level has to be regularly maintained, i.e. that of the crankcase. The crankcase filler-plug is on the top of the crankcase cover towards the front (a hexagon-shaped base with a domed, extended centre). The level plug is at the bottom, towards the rear and under the footrest (see Fig. 14). The drain

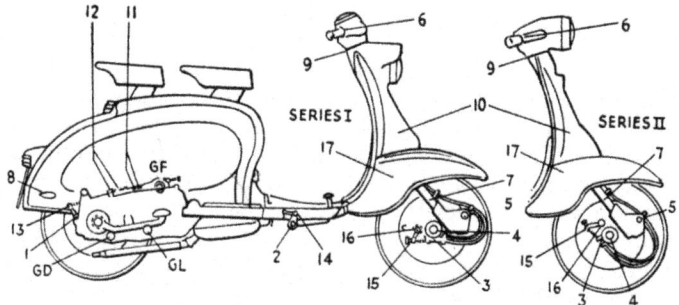

FIG. 13. LUBRICATION POINTS, Li 125 AND 150, SERIES I
AND SERIES II

(*See* table for key.)

TABLE

Grease	Oil
1. Rear-brake cam pin 2. Rear-brake pedal pin 3. Speedometer-box drive 4. Front-wheel bearing 5. Suspension box 6. Handlebar control-lever knuckles 7. Front-suspension springs 8. Side-panel clips 9. Steering bearing, upper 10. Steering bearing, lower	*Lubricate with oilcan and SAE 30 oil* 11. Clutch-cable knuckles 12. Gearchange knuckles 13. Rear-brake knuckles 14. Rear-brake pedal knuckle 15. Front-brake knuckle 16. Front-brake cam pin 17. Cable oilers (reached under front mudguard) *CRANKCASE OIL SAE* 90 GF—gearbox filler GL—gearbox level plug GD—gearbox drain plug

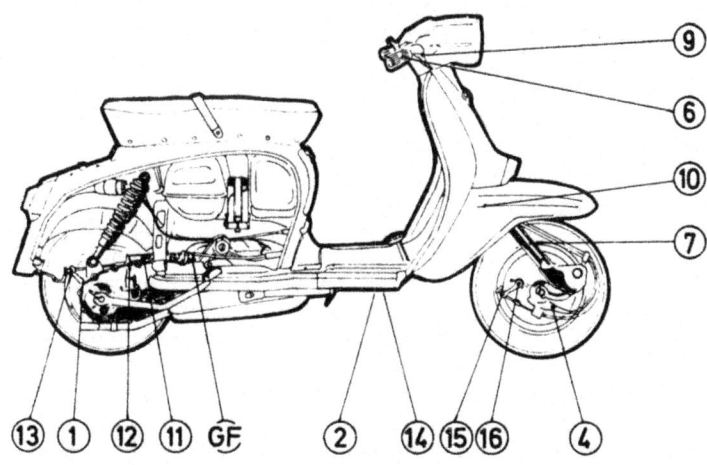

FIG. 14. LUBRICATION POINTS ON LATER MODELS

Points 1, 2, 4 and 16 may require grease-gun on some models; on
later models only point 1 is fitted with a grease nipple. All points
indicated are lubrication points, except *GF*, which is the gearbox filler.
(*See* table for key.)

plug is to the rear and just under the kick-starter spindle. The level and drain plugs may be identified by the hexagon-shaped socket in their top and are removed by unscrewing with a 10 mm hexagon spanner (supplied in the tool kit). It should be noted that the position of the drain and level plugs on the original Tv 175 model is different from that on the original Li models and all the Series II models (*see* Fig. 12).

For topping up the oil level, filler and level plugs are removed and SAE 90 oil poured in until it just begins to overflow from the level-plug opening. Both plugs are then replaced. To drain the crankcase completely (recommended after every 2,500 miles of running and after the first 500 or 1,000 miles in the case of new machines), all three plugs are removed, the oil which drains away being collected in a suitable container. This oil is waste and should be thrown away. Replace the drain plug before filling to level, as before. Flushing out before refilling is not necessary.

For all grease points lubricated by a grease gun, Energrease A1, or equivalent, is recommended. Two strokes of the gun should be adequate at all points, provided greasing is attended to on a regular schedule. It is important to avoid excessive application of grease to the rear-brake cam spindle on the rear of the crankcase casing as, otherwise, excess may get on to the brake linings and render the rear brake useless until it is stripped down and degreased completely. Grease-*packed* points, such as the front-wheel bearings, require a somewhat harder (higher melting-point) grease when repacked, such as Energrease L3, Castrolease WB, or equivalent.

All cables require regular oiling and special oilers are provided on the sheath where the group of cables bends round the main frame immediately by the front mudguard. The best method of applying oil to these points is to fit a short length of plastic tubing to a "Wesco" or similar type pressure oilcan, connect the end of the tubing to each cable nipple in turn and give four or five strokes on the oilcan trigger. If the model does not have oilers, oil must be applied directly to the bore of the outer sheath at a suitable end and distributed by manipulation of the inner cable.

The front-brake cable is not included in the group just described, as it emerges from the "run" at the first bend of the frame. The oiling point for this cable is by the clip on the front-suspension box. Other oiling points concern the main knuckle-joints as detailed in the lubrication diagrams. A particular virtue of the new models is that the number of lubrication points has been kept to a minimum and accessibility to them made somewhat simpler compared with earlier models.

Basic adjustments are simple and straightforward. All control cables have screw adjusters at the ends farthest from the handlebar controls, by means of which the tension of the cable can be increased (or decreased) as required. The handbrake cable should have a reasonable amount of slack movement but should take up smoothly and pull the front brake fully "on" before the limit of lever movement is reached, i.e. before the lever is pulled right in against the grip. The rear-brake pedal should have a generous amount of free travel to allow for any expansion of the brake backplate assembly.

The clutch requires regular adjustment to maintain a similar response from the clutch lever. The adjustment called for is that the clutch should just begin to slip when the clutch-lever movement corresponds to an opening, relative to the "wedge" formed with the housing of 1 to 2 millimetres (say about $\frac{1}{16}$ in.—see Fig. 19). Again the adjustment is done at the rear end of the clutch cable via the screw fitting.

The cables associated with the throttle and gear-change twist-grip controls should have no free play, but equally must not be in tension until the twist-grip is rotated. End-float on the twist-grips is governed by spacing washers between the cable pulley and its bearing. In the case of the throttle control, a friction-locking action is provided by a dished spring-washer inserted between the twist grip and the front-brake lever support.

On the electrical side the only item likely to require regular attention is the spark plug (also, where a battery is fitted, the electrolyte level should be checked regularly, see Chapter 10). Equivalent spark-plug types are detailed in the Specifications and Table 6. The plug used must be of the long-reach type. Choice of type may, however, be dictated by driving conditions. For slow driving, or a lot of idle running such as when the scooter is used in heavy traffic, a somewhat hotter-running plug may prove far less prone to fouling. Recommendations are summarized in Table 6. Plug gap, in all cases, should be set to approximately 0·020 (see page 34) and checked and reset at intervals of about 1,000 miles (when the plug would normally be removed for cleaning as a matter of routine maintenance in any case).

Timing should not need checking or altering as this is factory pre-set and fixed (see Chapters 9, 10, 11). A variation in contact-breaker gap can, however, affect the timing and also cause such faults as misfiring under load or difficult starting when the headlamp is switched on. Adjustment of the contact-breaker gap is carried out by removing the centre dust cover on the flywheel, when the points can be reached through one of the apertures in the flywheel.

On the original Tv 175 model the contact-point gap, full open, should be from 0·35–0·45 mm (15–20 thou.). If the gap is too large or too small it can be adjusted via the adjusting screw (see Fig. 40), although to gain access to the screw it is necessary for the flywheel to be removed. On the Li models no fixed gap can be given, the correct adjustment being that which gives separation of the points at the correct timing position. Increasing the gap in the open position will advance the separation point (relative to the fixed timing) and reducing the fully-open gap will retard it. Adjustment is, therefore, necessarily related to the correct timing position as given by the relative position of the flywheel (see Chapters 9 and 10). Adjustment of the point gap can be done with a screwdriver in all cases but Marelli points have an eccentric screw adjuster and the Filso points have a V-notch. The contact-breaker on the Ducati unit fitted to all Series II machines is adjusted by a screw (*see* Fig. 42).

Wheels are of the split-rim type and are interchangeable front and rear on all models. The front wheel can readily be removed with the machine pulled up on to its stand. To jack up sufficiently to remove the rear wheel, a special lift-stand is provided in the tool kit which fits into a lug in the bottom of the crankcase. Either wheel is then freed from the hub simply by

FIG. 15. DOMED NUTS (ARROWED) ARE FOR WHEEL REMOVAL.
GREASE NIPPLES SHOWN AT N

removing the four domed nuts. In the case of the front wheel, wheel and hub complete can be removed by loosening the two wheel nuts on the trailing links, loosening the front-brake cable clamp and disconnecting the trunnion from the brake lever on the backplate, and unscrewing the speedometer-drive locking ring and removing the cable. Then the handle-bars are turned to one side to drop out the wheel. Care must be taken not to pinch or kink the front-brake and speedometer-drive cables.

Wheel halves may be parted, e.g. to remove the tyre and tube, by unscrewing the four plain nuts holding the split rims together, but these nuts must never be undone whilst the tyre is inflated, otherwise the wheel halves will tend to fly apart with considerable force. Hence the importance of identifying the *domed* nuts as the correct ones to unscrew when removing a wheel.

For normal rear-wheel changing the retaining nuts can be tightened quite satisfactorily with the spanner provided in the tool kit. However, it is essential that if the rear hub be removed, when refitting it the retaining nut should be tensioned with a torque wrench with a setting of 120 lb/feet.

ROUTINE SERVICING

A more or less constant pattern of attention is required if any type of vehicle is to continue to give efficient, trouble-free service. Besides promoting consistent, smoother overall performance and reliability, adjustment and checking as specified ensure that any potential faults or troubles are detected and remedied at an early stage. Regular lubrication of all parts requiring attention ensures a full service life from all components. To neglect any item of routine servicing can prove, in the long run, an expensive business.

All the items detailed under this heading are well within the capabilities of any owner to perform, since no technical skill or knowledge is required to master the necessary actions. The time involved, too, is quite small. The expense of a complete oil change, recommended every 2,500 miles for

When	Parts concerned	Action
Weekly	Tyres Exterior	Check tyre pressures. Wash over with water and dry with chamois leather. *Note:* if hosing down, protect the air intake under the saddle against water getting in and entering the air filter.

Monthly or every 1,000 miles	Lubrication points (*see* Figs. 12–14).	Grease—rear-brake cam pin
		          rear-brake pedal pin
		          handlebar-lever knuckles.
		Oil—clutch-change knuckles
		       gear-change knuckles
		       rear-brake knuckle
		       front-brake knuckle
		       front-brake cam pin.

	Crankcase oil Brakes Clutch Spark plug Battery	Check level and top up as necessary. Check adjustment. Check adjustment. Remove and clean, check gap and adjust to 0·020-0·024 in. Check level of electrolyte and top up with distilled water if necessary. Grease battery terminals with "Vaseline."

Three monthly or every 2,500 miles
Note: these items in addition to normal monthly check due at this stage
	Lubrication points (*see* Figs. 12–14)
	Crankcase oil
	Clutch
	Flywheel-magneto
	Carburettor air filter
		Grease—front-wheel bearings (nipple)
		          suspension link boxes (nipple)
		          speedometer drive (nipple)
		Drain and refill.
		Adjust for 1/16 in. movement at handlebars.
		Oil felt pad lightly.
		Clean contact breaker points and adjust if necessary.
		Remove filter cartridge and clean by blowing through with low-pressure air (e.g. a tyre pump).

Six monthly or every 5,000 miles	Clean engine Decarbonize Steering head	Scrub or wash clean with petrol or paraffin and dry with clean rags. Decarbonize silencer, also cylinder head, cylinder and top of piston, as necessary (*see* Chapter 5). Adjust if necessary. Dismantle and repack with grease.

normal running, may be queried as unnecessary, but again is an economy in the long run. Oil does deteriorate, as well as get dirty, and lack of adequate lubrication is one of the most damaging things that can occur to a scooter. This applies just as much to cables (which can seize if not lubricated) as to the complete engine (which can be ruined by running on straight petrol instead of petrol/oil fuel.)

SPECIAL ATTENTION REQUIRED ON NEW MACHINES

On new machines particular care is called for as regards lubrication and adjustment over the first 2,000 miles. The following are points particularly specified as requiring attention—

After the first 250–300 miles	Complete lubrication service. Check and adjust all controls. Check steering adjustment. Check cylinder-head nuts and silencer ring-nut. Check wheel nuts and hub nuts (four plain, four domes each wheel). Check all other nuts and bolts. Check contact-breaker gap and points. Check handlebar fixing-clamp.
After the first 1,000 miles	Normal lubrication check, but crankcase engine-oil drained and refilled. Adjust gear-change and clutch cables. Check correct engagement of all gears. Adjust brakes. Check Duplex transmission chain. Clean petrol-tap filter. Check spark plug, clean and adjust gap as necessary. Check lighting circuit, generator charge and condition of battery. Adjust headlamp beam, if necessary.
After the first 1,500–2,000 miles	Decarbonize silencer. Check and adjust front and rear suspension. Check and adjust steering. Check and adjust carburettor.

TABLE 6

RECOMMENDED PLUG TYPES

Note: Spark plug gap should be 0·020–0·24 in. for earlier models with four-pole magnetos; and 0·018–0·020 in. for later models with six-pole magnetos.

	Champion	K.L.G.	Lodge
Normal running . .	N4	FE75	CLNH
Slow driving or novices .	N5 or N84	FE75	CLNH
Prolonged fast driving .	N3	FE80	CLNP

Note: For Series III machines and the GT 200 recommended plugs are—for running-in: heat range 225 Bosch scale; after running-in: heat range 226 to 240 Bosch scale, according to conditions of use.

4 Fault-finding

ALL Lambretta models are basically trouble-free in operation and the Li and Tv models even more so than earlier models because of developments and improvements in design layout. If a fault does develop it is most likely to be due to the owner not following proper instructions, abusing the machine unduly or neglecting routine maintenance. Unless the correct four per cent oil/petrol mixture is used, serious and permanent damage can result to the engine yet this is a point which, surprisingly enough, many new owners ignore. The fact that oil is added to the engine crankcase does *not* mean that the engine itself is lubricated as a normal car engine. The scooter engine depends entirely on oil being mixed with the petrol fuel to lubricate the cylinder, piston and crankshaft.

Regular attention to lubrication and adjustment of other parts, as detailed in Chapter 3, merely underlines the truth of the old adage that "a stitch in time saves nine," only in this case regular attention eliminates the possibility of faults occurring, or at least serves to check possible faults at an early stage before they have become serious and expensive to put right. Most of the simpler faults which can develop may be readily traced and put right by the average owner. Only those brought on by normal wear after long use may demand the attention of a specialized mechanic and, even then, many of the jobs involved can be tackled by anyone with a certain flair for mechanical work, following the detailed instructions given in the remaining chapters.

The weakest link, and virtually the only weak link, is the spark plug, which has to work under most arduous conditions and is subject to fouling. This can reach a point where the gap is bridged or completely fouled so that a spark can no longer be generated across the gap, when there is nothing to fire the mixture; hence the engine stops. There is also the possibility of the spark-plug gap "growing" so that the gap eventually becomes too large for the spark to jump satisfactorily. Although the magneto coil is capable of providing enough high-tension current to jump a gap of about $\frac{5}{16}$ in., conditions inside the cylinder head, where the gas mixture is under compression, are far less favourable than in "free air" and so an excessive spark-plug gap, although still within the nominal limit of the spark, may produce intermittent firing. Dirty, pitted or badly adjusted contact-breaker points may also detract from the spark performance. Incorrectly adjusted points can also affect the timing, or the instant at which the spark appears in the cylinder.

The manner in which the scooter is handled can also affect the susceptibility of the plug to fouling. The worst conditions are a considerable amount of slow running and idling where the plug never gets quite hot enough to remain dry and reasonably clean. If the plug is removed and examined it will be found covered with a dark, rather oily coating, with a tendency to foul at an early stage. In such cases a change of plug to a type which runs hotter may be beneficial (see Chapter 3 and Table 6).

Normally, a correct plug should give at least 500 miles' running without trouble, at which stage it should be removed for cleaning and checking as a matter of routine maintenance. It may well be that the same plug would run for much longer periods without giving trouble, but neglecting plug maintenance, which is so simple anyway, is a foolish policy. The actual working life of the plug is also a variable factor. Some plugs will apparently last indefinitely. Other scooter riders prefer to fit a new plug regularly, some after every 1,000 miles. The cost of a new plug is quite low and regular replacement is usually a wise policy. Equally, one should always carry a new (or at least properly cleaned) spare plug to refit at any time, should the need occur. This will be a much simpler operation than trying to clean a fouled plug on the spot, usually without any suitable tools.

Possible starting and running faults are discussed under typical headings below. The majority are not machine faults so much as those of faulty maintenance or operation. Definite mechanical faults may first show up as a rattle or unusual noise and anything of this nature requires investigating immediately, before the fault has had time to develop into anything serious. Squeaking noises are generally a sign of lack of lubrication somewhere; rattles are an indication that something is working loose. Neither can be expected to correct itself without attention and the longer they are left the worse they can become.

Certain noises are inherent in the operation of the scooter and do not indicate maladjustment or a mechanical fault. A certain amount of rattle may be heard from the piston, for example, until the engine has warmed up. On the other hand, a rattling from the kick-starter end will almost certainly indicate that the ratchet has not properly disengaged and calls for immediate attention. On the Series I Tv 175 there may also be a distinct rattle from the torque damper and transmission at low idling speeds. If this disappears when the clutch lever is lifted, this is quite normal and can be ignored. Other features which may cause worry, such as a vibration on the gear-change twist grip, can often be eliminated by a simple modification. The local Lambretta service agent should be consulted on such a point, or on any point of doubt where a mechanical fault is suspected, and one's experience and knowledge are not adequate to trace and deal with it.

STARTING AND RUNNING FAULTS

Symptom	Cause	Remedy
Engine fails to start	Electrical fault	Remove and check the spark plug. Clean if dirty and check and reset the gap, if necessary. If the plug is very wet, this is an indication of excessive use of the choke. Dry the plug off by blowing and turn the engine over several times to blow out excess mixture before replacing the plug. If the plug appears in order, check that a spark is generated across the gap by holding against the cylinder with high-tension lead attached and spin the engine over. If no spark occurs at the plug gap, check the lead separately and see if a spark jumps from the end to the cylinder or frame of the machine over a gap of not more than $\frac{1}{4}$ in. This will "prove" the plug one way or the other. If no spark is produced by the lead, the contact-breaker points are probably dirty, pitted or badly adjusted, and need attention.
	Lack of fuel	Check if tap is turned on and if there is fuel in the tank. Fuel line may be blocked, filter choked or carburettor jets blocked. Choke not operated properly; check cable and operation on carburettor.
	Excess fuel	Choke left closed too long; treat as for "wet" plug above. When restarting, close fuel tap and turn choke off and kick over with throttle well open. Carburettor float sticking (carburettor not vertical), or float damaged.
Engine stops immediately after starting	Lack of fuel	Requires choke to start. If choke is operated, check as above.
	Electrical fault	Spark plug fouled by deposit on top of cylinder thrown on to plug. Disconnected high-tension lead.
Engine runs badly at idling speed	Carburettor	Incorrect slow-running adjustment. Readjust when the engine is warm. Dirt in carburettor, causing wrong mixture. Air leaks on manifold causing too weak a mixture.
	Ignition	Plug gap incorrect. Check and readjust to 0·020–0·024 in. gap (0·018–0·020 in. on later models) Contact-breaker incorrectly adjusted or faulty.
	Fuel mixture	Wrong mixture; too much, or too little, oil.
Idling speed changes when machine is moved from its stand	Control Cable	If this occurs, suspect the throttle cable as being too tight. Free the throttle cable outer from its retaining clips and see if this cures the fault.

STARTING AND RUNNING FAULTS—(contd.)

Symptom	Cause	Remedy
Engine misfires under load	Ignition	Spark plug gap too large. Spark plug fouled and needs cleaning. Contact-breaker gap needs adjustment, or timing is incorrect (also caused by wrong contact-breaker gap adjustment). Contact-breaker points dirty.
	Fuel	Wrong mixture (too lean). Check that fuel mixture is correct. Check if carburettor needle is damaged or worn. Try in a different position. Partial blockage in fuel line of carburettor. Check and clean, as necessary.
	Air leaks	Check carburettor manifold and hose joints for tightness. An air leak will cause an excessively weak mixture.
Lack of pulling power when running	Timing	Timing too far retarded, which may be caused by faulty setting of the contact-breaker gap or faulty positioning of the stator plate.
	Air leaks	Check as above. Also check cylinder-head nuts for tightness.
	Coking up	Cylinder head, exhaust port and/or silencer may require decarbonizing.
Knocking noise from engine	Timing	Ignition too far advanced, due to incorrect contact-breaker gap or stator plate being moved from correct position.
	Pre-ignition	Most probably caused by carbon deposits in the cylinder head, calling for decarbonizing. Can also be caused by a dirty spark plug.
	Fuel mixture	Incorrect fuel mixture in tank. Check carburettor for cleanliness and setting of needle.
Engine does not "two-stroke" properly at certain throttle openings	Mixture	Check carburettor and particularly the position of the needle.
Engine noisy (general)	Wear or mechanical fault developing	Try to trace the region from which the noise is coming. A different noise from normal engine noise is usually an indication of something faulty or coming loose and should be attended to at once.
Rattles and general noise	Fastenings working loose	Trace the region from which the noise is coming and look for loose fastenings, etc. When retightening, check that spring washers, etc. are located under nuts (where called for). Rusted threads can, where necessary, be eased with freeing oil.

FAULTS PECULIAR TO THE NEW MODELS

The following are some of the more unusual faults which may be experienced with the Li and Tv models, some of which can be extremely puzzling to trace, should they occur—

Engine will not start with headlamp switched on. Almost invariably due to wrong contact-breaker setting giving incorrect timing and weak spark. A weak spark can also result from using a Filso magneto with any other than a Filso high-tension coil (the other magnetos are far less critical as to the type of high-tension coil used).

Engine stops suddenly, when running well, for no apparent reason. This can be caused by a pillion passenger's clothing obscuring the carburettor air intake on Li models (the intake being located between the saddles). It can also occur, but is less likely, on Tv models where the air intake is at the rear.

Series II models incorporate a disc valve at the base of the air-intake hose. If this valve is displaced from its housing (in the rubber hose) it can be sucked up into the carburettor to stop the engine. When the engine stops, the displaced valve drops back into place, and it can be most puzzling to trace what is happening.

Silencer blocked-up. Thick, oily deposits in the silencer causing partial blockage and loss of power can be caused by a faulty crankcase oil-seal letting oil get into the exhaust.

Exhaust gasket wrong way round. Should the exhaust pipe be disconnected for any reason, it is relatively easy to replace the exhaust gasket the wrong way round, causing partial blockage and loss of power.

High-tension lead frayed or broken. On some models the high-tension lead is rather short and continual movement of the engine can fray the insulation, leading to a weak or intermittent spark. This fault is usually obvious on examination.

Broken clutch cable. On Series I models the trunnion is sometimes too tight a fit in the lever, so that it never seats home properly. Thus the cable is subjected to continual bending instead of a push-pull action and can break at an early stage. Check that the trunnion fits home properly, filing out the housing as necessary.

Choke remaining operated. If the carburettor is dismantled or the choke cable removed, it is possible to replace with the choke remaining in a closed or partly closed position, regardless of the position of the choke control. As a result, the carburettor continues to supply an over-rich mixture when running.

5 Detailed maintenance (general)

THIS chapter covers detailed maintenance, disassembly, etc. of all main items other than the engine group. The description can be taken as applying to all models except that minor differences and detail amendments may be encountered on later models. Where there are distinct differences involved, these are noted.

The standard kit of tools supplied with each new machine is detailed in Table 7. Special tools applicable to workshop use or extensive home maintenance are detailed in Table 8. These are mostly concerned with disassembly and reassembly of the engine-group components although some are required for detailed maintenance of the steering head and front suspension. It should be noted that some of the workshop tools are common to the Lambretta LD models as well as the Tv and Li series.

BRAKES

In the case of the front wheel (Fig. 16), separation of the wheel from the hub (after removal from the front suspension) is accomplished by unscrewing the off-side spindle-nut and the 19 mm nut beneath and driving the spindle through with a mallet or "soft" hammer. The rear hub is disassembled simply by undoing the 27 mm centre nut, leaving the wheel attached, and knocking the off-side of the *tyre* hard to force off. The same procedure applies in reassembly, knocking against the tyre (from the on-side) to force back in place rather than relying entirely on the tightening of the nut to draw the wheel back into position. An appreciable amount of side-play on the rear-wheel is correct and not a fault due to wear.

Brake components are illustrated in Fig. 17. When reassembling, pivots and cams should be lightly greased, and care taken not to get any grease on the brake linings. If the brake linings are greasy or oily they should be cleaned thoroughly with carbon tetrachloride (e.g. "Thawpit" or "Pyrene"). The surface of the linings should *not* be roughened with a file or coarse emery.

Detail changes which occur on the Series I Tv 175 affect the spring washer on the rear-wheel nut (prior to No. 1457), and the helical pinion and gear for the speedometer drive on the front wheel (prior to No. 1250). A grease nipple was also fitted to lubricate the rear-brake cam but omitted on the Li and all Series II machines. The illustration shows the assemblies used throughout the Series II machines.

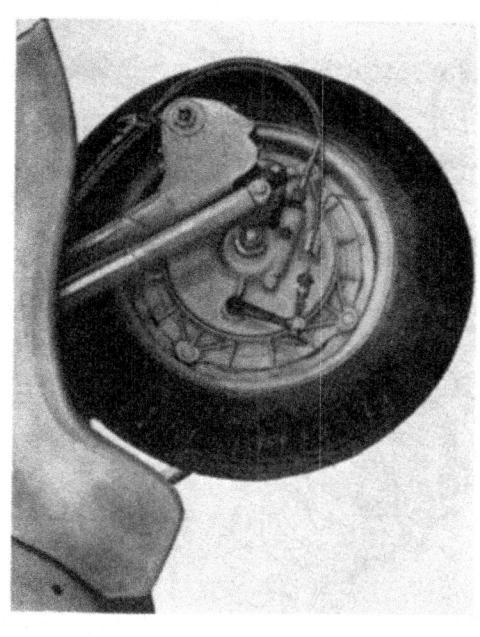

Fig. 16. Li Front Suspension (Left) and Tv Front Suspension (Right) are Basically Similar but not Interchangeable

No provision is made for fitting shock absorber on Li models and there are other detail differences. To fit shock absorber on Li models demands welded-on lugs.

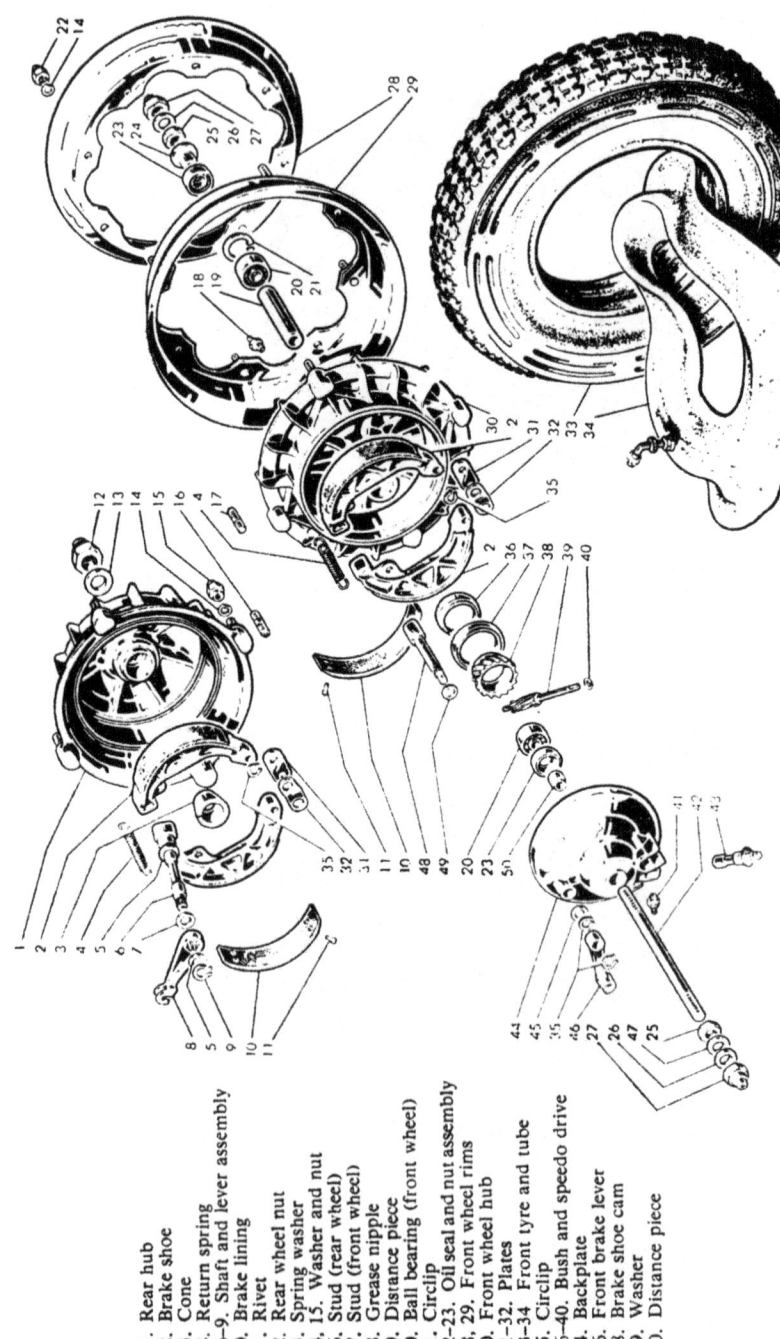

1. Rear hub
2. Brake shoe
3. Cone
4. Return spring
6–9. Shaft and lever assembly
10. Brake lining
11. Rivet
12. Rear wheel nut
13. Spring washer
14, 15. Washer and nut
16. Stud (rear wheel)
17. Stud (front wheel)
18. Grease nipple
19. Distance piece
20. Ball bearing (front wheel)
21. Circlip
22–23. Oil seal and nut assembly
28, 29. Front wheel rims
30. Front wheel hub
31–32. Plates
33–34. Front tyre and tube
35. Circlip
36–40. Bush and speedo drive
44. Backplate
46. Front brake lever
48. Brake shoe cam
49. Washer
50. Distance piece

FIG. 17. FRONT- AND REAR-BRAKE ASSEMBLIES. BRAKE LININGS ARE BONDED TO SHOES AND ALSO SECURED WITH TWO RIVETS AT EACH END

The Series III 175 (Slimstyle) and GT 200 models are fitted with a disc front brake as standard, operated by a ball and cam plate via a conventional front brake cable. This type of brake has the advantage of eliminating brake "fade" at high speeds and "locking" at low speeds, particularly on wet roads.

The actual brake assembly includes a central disc which engages on three pins on the wheel and thus rotates with the wheel, with one fixed brake pad and one sliding brake pad mounted on each side of the disc. When the brake lever is operated the sliding pad is pressed against the disc which in turn moves sideways and is pressed against the fixed pad. The disc, and thus the wheel, is thereby clamped between the two pads to provide the braking action.

The brake lining thickness is approximately 5 mm and the pads should be replaced when wear has reduced this thickness to about 3 mm. The setting of the fixed pads is adjustable by a stud and locknut, accessible from the left-hand side. Readjustment is called for when the angle between the brake operating lever and the cable is more than 90 degrees. This is done by completely removing the cable from the operating lever, then slackening the nut on the fixed pad side with a ring spanner. The stud inside this nut can then be tightened with a 4 mm Allen key, taking this up until the front wheel is locked. The stud should then be unscrewed one turn and the nut tightened to lock the pad in this position. The control cable is then replaced and adjusted by means of the knurled screw.

CONTROL CABLES

Control-cable installation applicable to all Li Series models is shown in Fig. 18. The upper terminations of the gear-change and throttle cables are exposed by removing the central handlebar-fairing, held by two screws on the underside. Removal of these screws allows the fairing to be lifted up to give access to the speedometer cable at its junction with the speedometer head. The knurled nut can then be turned to release the speedometer cable and the base, freeing the fairing and allowing the speedometer to be detached.

To replace cable inners, all cables except the throttle cable can be freed at their lower end and drawn out from the handlebar end In the case of the throttle cable, the nipple at the lower end must be unsoldered first. New cables can be fed back from the handlebar end. In the case of the front-brake and clutch cables, the lever pivot-nut is removed and the lever pulled away from the handlebar with the cable attached. A new throttle cable can be fitted with a cable connector of the type fitted to the clutch cable in place of the soldered nipple, when replaced. Alternatively, the only other satisfactory solution is to replace the throttle cable and outer complete as a unit, which means that the headlamp and headlamp casing or front fairing must be removed (Series I or II, respectively).

The headlamp and headlamp casing (Series I) or front fairing complete

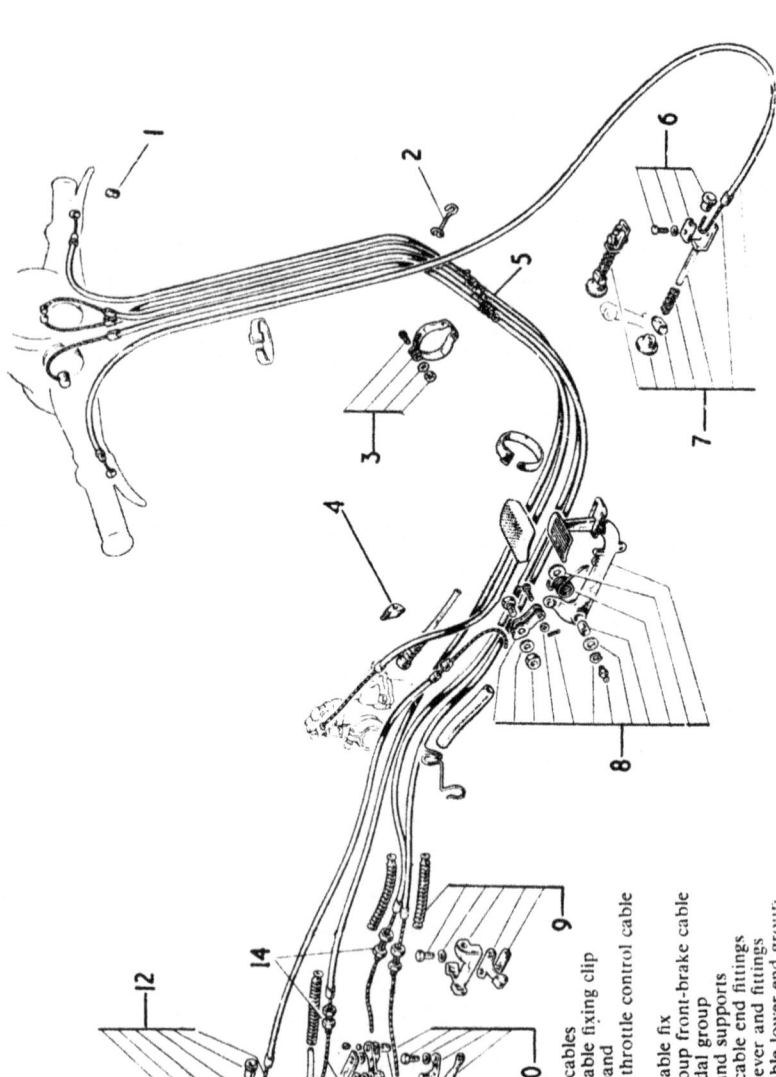

FIG. 18. CONTROL-CABLE LAYOUT, ALL MODELS

1. Trunnion for cables
2. Front-brake cable fixing clip
3. Cable fixing-band
4. Grommet for throttle control cable
5. Cable oilers
6. Front-brake cable fix
7. Lower end group front-brake cable
8. Footbrake pedal group
9. Cable plates and supports
10. Gear-change cable end fittings
11. Gear-change lever and fittings
12. Rear-brake cable lower end group
13. Adjuster clamp for rear-brake cable
14. Adjuster screws and nuts

(Series II) must be removed for replacing cable outers, positioning and fastening being obvious (*see* Fig. 18). When replacing a cable only, it should be noted that in the case of the clutch and front-brake cables only the respective hand-lever need be detached, but where the throttle or gear-change cable is to be replaced, the main handlebar-fairing must be removed, as described above.

On later models there is a small recess in each lever which houses a small

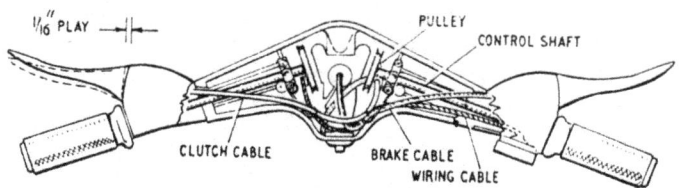

FIG. 19. LAYOUT OF HANDLEBAR CONTROL SHAFTS AND PULLEYS AND CABLING

Note: the arrangement of cables differs slightly on different models.

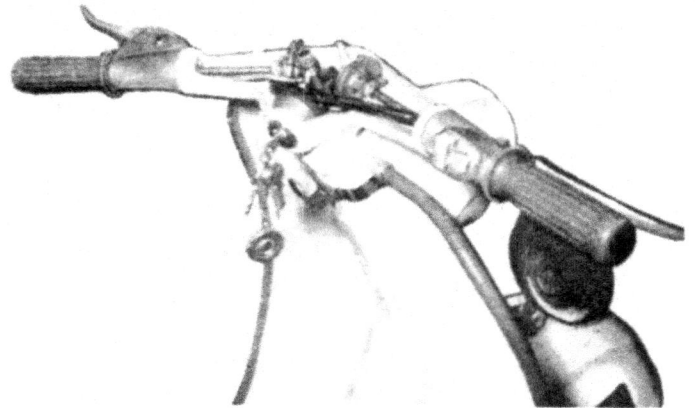

FIG. 19a. HANDLEBAR GROUP, TV 175 SERIES I

spring with a plastic cap, the purpose of which is to eliminate vibration of the lever by providing spring-damping. When removing the pivot lever it is important to do this slowly so that the spring and cap can be captured safely and not allowed to fly out, when they can easily be lost. When replacing clutch and brake cables on early models, check that the trunnion fits properly home in the lever, if necessary enlarging the hole slightly with a file. If the trunnion rides out of its proper position, early breakage of the cable will result.

Removal of the handlebar-fairing is also necessary to gain access to the throttle and gear-change control shafts (Fig. 19). These shafts are rotated

by the respective twist grips and transmit the necessary linear motion to
the cables via pulleys at their inner ends. End-float on the twist grips is
governed by spacing washers on the control rod and can be adjusted by
slackening the pinchbolt and moving the twist grip inwards or outwards
slightly, as required, before tightening the pinchbolt again. If it is necessary
to replace a control shaft, the pinchbolt is slackened right off, or removed,
when the shaft itself can be tapped out from the centre with a suitable

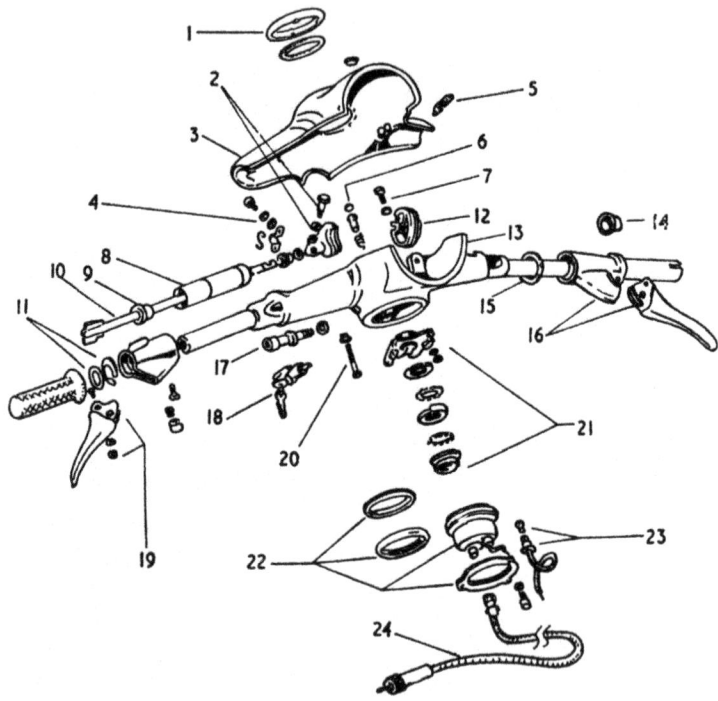

FIG. 20. HANDLEBAR GROUP IN DETAILS
APPLICABLE TO ALL MODELS IN GENERAL DETAIL,
BUT SERIES II LAYOUT SHOWN

1. Speedometer housing
2. Throttle-shaft clamp assembly
3. Upper handlebar fairing
4. Fixing-plate assembly
5. Gasket
6. Steering-lock disc, pin and spring
7. Handlebar fixing-screw and washer
8. Throttle-control sleeve
9. Anti-vibration bush
10. Throttle-control shaft
11. Twist grip and washers
12. Gear-change pulley
13. Handlebar unit (different for Li and Tv)
14. Anti-vibration bush
15. Thrust washer
16. Clutch lever and housing
17. Handlebar fixing-screw
18. Steering lock
19. Front-brake lever assembly
20. Handlebar fixing-screw and spring-washer
21. Clamp and race assembly
22. Speedometer cover and gasket
23. Speedometer bulb and cable
24. Speedometer drive cable

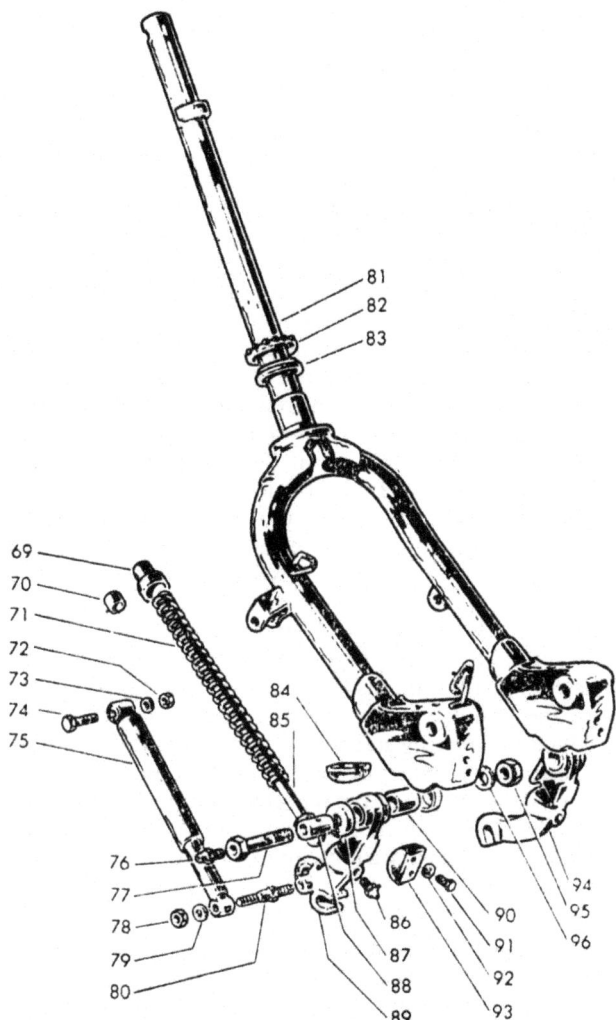

FIG. 21. FRONT-FORK ASSEMBLY
(BASICALLY SIMILAR ON ALL MODELS)

69–71. Suspension spring assembly
72–75. Shock absorber (Tv 175 only)
81. Front fork (different for Li and Tv models)
82. Ball race, lower
83. Cone, for lower ball race
84. Plate, with rebound buffer for suspension spring
85. Piston, for guiding suspension spring
86. Grease nipple, for trailing link
87. Greaser caps

88. Pin, for trailing link
89. Trailing link, right hand (different for Li and Tv models)
90. Bush, for trailing link
91. Screw, fixing plate
92. Spring washer
93. Plate, with rebound buffer
94. Trailing link, left hand, (different for Li and Tv models)
95. Nut, for screws at Fig. 77
96. Spring washer, for nuts at Fig. 95

Note. The main difference on Series III models (and GT 200) is that the handlebar clamp pinchbolt groove is cut into the nearside of the fork stem in a fore-and-aft direction, this bolt being approached for disassembly from the headlamp assembly punch. Front-brake and clutch cables will have to be released at their lower end to allow the necessary freedom of movement. The clutch-lever support will fall free when the shaft is withdrawn but the front-brake support will remain fixed to the handlebars. It can be detached by unscrewing the two locking screws holding it in place. Before attempting to remove the shaft, however, the twist grips should be *pushed* off by pressure on the inner lip (never *pulled* off). Details of the handlebar group are given in Fig. 20.

If it is necessary to remove the handlebars, the central fairing member must first be detached, as described previously, when the screw fixing the handlebars to the steering tube can be removed and the handlebars tapped upwards lightly with a mallet to free. The complete handlebar assembly can then be laid carefully to the front (Series II) or back (Series I), supported on the control cables. It will be necessary to undo the frame clamp to get the required play. The steering adjustment ring is exposed on top of the steering tube. If this ring is unscrewed and the ball-race removed, the front fork can be slid out complete (provided the cables are detached from the lower end).

Adjustment of the steering-head bearings is provided by the ring nuts, which require special tools for proper tightening. They should be tightened up until the steering still remains free but has no up-and-down movement. Alignment of the handlebars and front wheel is simply governed by the position in which the locking screw is tightened when reassembling. If it is necessary to adjust alignment, this screw is slackened off (as in detaching the handlebars), the position of the handlebars adjusted and then tightened up again. Finally, the main handlebar-fairing is replaced, taking care to ensure that the control and wiring cables are not trapped or forced into sharp bends.

FRONT SUSPENSION

The front suspension is shown in Fig. 21. The only difference between models is that the 175 c.c. and 200 c.c. machines incorporate a hydraulic shock absorber for damping. Also, in the case of the Li Series, early models had two tubes brazed into a forged lug at the base of the steering column, changed on later models to a single U-shaped tube welded to a pressed stem bracket. The latter type only is now available as a replacement part, which calls for the use of some additional parts if it is to be fitted as a replacement to an earlier model.

Dismantling and reassembly is fairly straightforward, first detaching the brake cable from the wheel, unscrewing the speedometer drive and detaching the drive box and removing the wheel. The pivot pin on the trailing link can be removed by unscrewing the 19 mm fixing nut and the buffer prised out after removing the fixing screws and the grease nipple under the lever. A special tool is required to compress the suspension spring before the trailing links can be detached. The springs, pistons and piston guide-rings can then be withdrawn. It may be necessary to fish for the latter with a piece of wire bent over at the end. Reassembly follows the reverse order.

On later models the link has a loose ball for seating and no grease nipple. In this case no spring compressor tool is needed. After the pivot bolt nut, washer and cable clip have been removed a box spanner can be placed over the outer end of the wheel spindle slot to apply leverage to the link so that the rebound buffer can be levered out with a screwdriver. The link can then be released, the pivot bolt removed, and the remainder of the assembly dismantled. The pivot bush parts are identical on all models.

FUEL TANK

The fuel-tank installation and its relationship to the air-filter, carburettor, fuel-tap and choke controls is shown in Figs. 22 and 23. The filter element can readily be withdrawn for cleaning at regular intervals, when it should be shaken and blown through, never washed in water or petrol. There is a considerable difference in the arrangement of the ducting and the filter design on the Series I models (different again between the Li and the Tv) and the Series II machines (see Figs. 7 and 8). In the former case, the filter is accessible from the left under the tool locker, covered by a circular metal plate. On all Series II and III models the air-filter element is directly accessible from the left-hand side immediately in front of the tank by unscrewing the oval-shaped metal "elbow" at the end of the hose (held by a central thumbscrew).

To remove the tank (Series I machines) it is first necessary to remove the battery and its support straps. The air-induction tube must be withdrawn from the air chamber by slackening the clamp and pulling free. The petrol feed-pipe can then be detached from the carburettor and the tank drained dry. Then remove the petrol-tap control rod by extracting its pin and the petrol tap from the tank. The tank can then be freed by removing the supporting straps and withdrawn by rotating in a clockwise direction from the flywheel side of the machine.

On Series II and III models the procedure for removing the tank is essentially similar except that the air-filter box has to be removed first to allow space for the tank to be withdrawn.

DECARBONIZING

No definite rules can be given as to when decarbonizing is required, since much depends on how the machine is driven. Carbon deposits accumulate more readily when an engine is run slowly with little or no full-throttle work. The cumulative effect of carbon deposits in the exhaust system results in a gradual blockage of the passages, producing back-pressure and loss of power and engine efficiency. Carbon deposits inside the engine, i.e. on the top of the piston and in the top part of the cylinder (the combustion chamber or cylinder head), may be heated up to the point where localized "hot spots" are developed with the engine running, causing

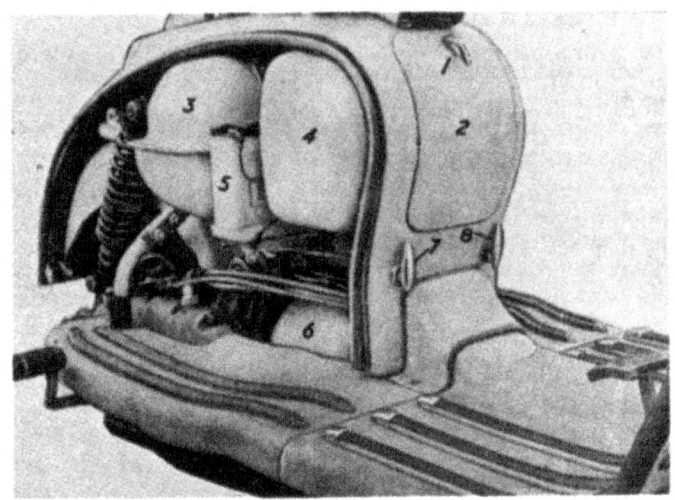

FIG. 22. DISPOSITION OF COMPONENTS ON SERIES II MACHINES

1. Handle and lock for tool locker
2. Tool locker (door opens downwards)
3. Fuel tank
4. Tool locker
5. Battery
6. Cylinder enclosed within cowl
7. Choke
8. Fuel tap

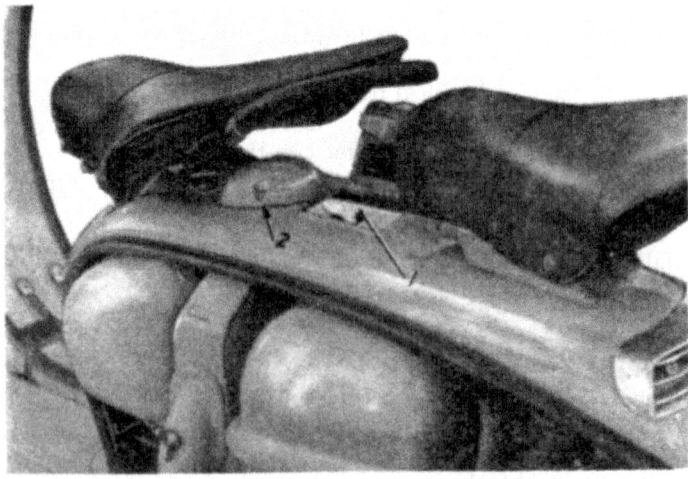

FIG. 23. FUEL-TANK FILLER (1) IS REACHED VIA HINGED FLAP
BETWEEN SADDLES ON LI MODELS. ONE-PIECE SADDLE PIVOTS
FORWARDS ON TV MODELS

Note: carburettor air intake (2) on Li models. This can be accidentally
blanked off by pillion passenger's clothing unless care is taken to leave
it free.

pre-ignition of the fuel by acting as effective "spark plugs" to fire the mixture before the proper spark initiates combustion at the proper part of the working cycle.

The silencer normally carbons up faster than the cylinder; so decarbonizing the silencer, or cleaning out carbon deposit, is usually called for before complete decarbonizing is required, and the improvement in performance resulting from clearing a partially-blocked silencer can be quite considerable.

Decarbonizing is not a skilled job and may well be tackled by the average owner (particularly decarbonizing the silencer). As a general rule, full decarbonizing should never be required under 5,000 miles and on a machine normally driven fairly hard, and with correct fuel mixture, probably not before 10,000 miles. The silencer may well benefit from decarbonizing at an earlier stage, however, particularly if a loss of power is being experienced which cannot be traced to any definite fault.

The silencer unit is attached by three nuts on the crankcase cover. To remove it, it is first necessary to unscrew the two nuts holding the right-hand footboard to the frame, the screw fixing the frame connecting-piece and the two screws fixing the footboard bracket so that the footboard can be detached. The silencer can then be removed, unscrewing the clamp to detach the exhaust tube from the cylinder. The tailpipe can then be

TABLE 7
STANDARD TOOL KITS

	Series I Li	Series I Tv 175	Series II Models
Spark plug/wheel nut spanner . .	14–21 mm cranked box	14–21 mm cranked box	14–21 mm cranked box
Crankcase plug spanner	10 mm hexagon	10 mm hexagon	10 mm hexagon
Rear-wheel nut spanner	14–27 mm	14–27 mm	14–27 mm
G. P. spanner . .	8 × 10 mm flat	8 × 10 mm flat	8 × 10 mm flat
Screwdriver . .	Yes	Yes	Yes
Rear-wheel stand .	Yes	Yes	Yes
Points file . . .	Yes	Yes	Yes
Allen key . . .	3·5 mm	3·5 mm	3·5 mm

Note. Series III and GT 200 kits are identical except for the inclusion of an 8 mm Allen key to the front fork pinchbolt.

detached from the silencer body. On Series III models there is an additional bracket underneath the silencer with a bolt screwing upwards into the crankcase. Silencer fixings also differ on the J Series and Starstream models, but the method of attachment and removal is obvious.

On the Tv 175 Series I a plug is fitted to the silencer body which can be removed to inspect the interior. Li Series I and all Series II machines have a different shape of silencer without this inspection plug. Both tailpipe and silencer body should be cleaned and scraped free of carbon deposits as far as possible, although the recommended procedure is to use a blowlamp flame, or similar, to burn off and loosen the carbon deposits from the silencer body so that they can be shaken out.

Silencers fitted to Li Series III and J Series models cannot be cleaned and can only be replaced if they become coked up. This should not happen in less than 15,000 miles with normal running, and may be very much longer.

On reassembly it is an advantage to smear the exhaust-tube end with heat-resistant metallic sealer (e.g. Bostonia No. 3) to ensure a gas-tight joint at this point. It is not necessary to seal the tailpipe into the silencer body.

Complete decarbonizing can be carried out without removing the engine from the frame. The silencer unit is detached, as just described, along with the spark plug, carburettor and air hose. If the two 24 mm nuts holding the suspension unit are now removed and the unit slid off, the engine unit will pivot to drop the cylinder below the frame, when the cylinder cowling can be removed. Access is now given to the upper part of the exhaust pipe which can be detached at its flange fixing to the cylinder (Series I models) by removing the two brass nuts. The cylinder head and cylinder barrel can be withdrawn by unscrewing the head nuts, but *see* Chapters 6 and 7 for specific details of disassembly of the engine.

Carbon deposits should be scraped off the cylinder head and piston top and the exhaust port in the cylinder wall using a soft tool, but not a knife which could score and damage the engine units. Care should be taken not to drop deposits into the crankcase. If the piston is removed it is important to note that the piston-ring pegs are located on either side of the exhaust port on the Li engines, and on the *upper* side of the piston in the case of the Tv 175 Series I.

The fitting of the exhaust tube to the cylinder is also different on Series I and Series II Tv 175 models. Flange fitting, with a gasket, is standard on all Li models and Series II Tv 175, but the Series I Tv 175 has a ring-nut fitting (requiring a C-spanner to manipulate) and a circular gasket. Although similar in form, the exhaust-pipe, silencer and tailpipe units are different on all Series II models, compared with Series I Li models, whilst the Series I Tv 175 components are different throughout.

The ease with which the silencer can be removed, and the best way of going about it, varies with different models. On early models, where the

TABLE 8

SPECIAL TOOLS

Tool Part No.	Description	Applicable on Models
0517/C	Electrical timing indicator	All Models
37058	Flywheel extractor	All Models
37276	Flywheel-nut spanner	Li 125, Tv Series I
39847	Piston-ring clip	Li 125, Li 150, Tv 175
40482	Steering-race cup spanner	All Models
40490	Steering-lock ring spanner	All Models
49188	Flywheel flange extractor	All Models
49194	Piston-ring clip	Li 125, Li 150, Tv 175
49221	Connecting-rod holding tool	Li models, Tv models
52150	Flywheel-nut box spanner	Li models, Tv Series II
54362	Small-end bush reamer	All Models
56686	Clutch-compressor tool	Tv Series I
57836	Handlebar-lock spanner	All Models
57865	Drive-chain alignment tool	All Models
58013	Flywheel holding tool	All Models
58021	Front fork spring-loading tool	All Models
58873	Small-end extractor and reamer	All Models
59170	Crankshaft inner race extractor	Li and Series II models, Tv Series I
59328	Inner clutch bell-housing extractor	Li models, Tv Series II
59329	Crankshaft ball-bearing extractor	Li models, Tv Series II
59350	Needle bearing outer race extractor	Li models, Tv Series II
59351	Clutch circlip fitting tool	Li models, Tv Series II
59804	Clutch-bell housing locking tool	Li models, Tv Series II
59826	Rear-wheel extractor	Li models, Tv Series II
60051	Shock absorber sleeve extractor	Li models, Tv Series II
60405	Rear-wheel bearing punch	Li models, Tv Series II

exhaust pipe connects to the silencer near the silencer body, it is easiest to detach the silencer first. On later models, where the joint comes nearer the engine because of the longer pipe on the silencer, better access is given by removing the right-hand footboard first. On later models, too, the engine cowling cannot be completely removed until the exhaust pipe is detached from the engine, first loosening the cowl and sliding down the pipe, then detaching the pipe from the cylinder and finally sliding the cowl off the pipe.

6 TV 175 Series I Engine Group

LAYOUT of the engine group of the Series I model is shown in Fig. 24. The clutch is mounted on the engine crankshaft and the primary drive is taken by Duplex chain via a sprocket and pinion, a further gear behind the sprocket (larger wheel) engaging a gear drive on the gearbox mainshaft.

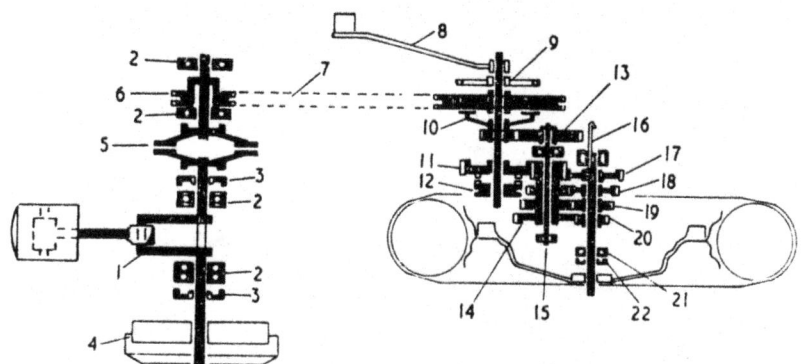

FIG. 24. LAYOUT OF TV 175 SERIES I ENGINE GROUP

1. Crankshaft
2. Ball-bearing
3. Oil seal
4. Flywheel magneto
5. Clutch
6. Sprocket
7. Duplex-chain primary drive
8. Kick-starter pedal arm
9. Return spring for kick-starter arm
10. Torque damper
11. Kick-starter pinion
12. Kick-starter ratchet
13. Geardrive on mainshaft
14. Main gear group
15. Transmission shaft
16. Cursor for gear-selector shaft
17. Layshaft first gear
18. Layshaft second gear
19. Layshaft third gear
20. Layshaft fourth gear
21. Ball-bearing
22. Oil-seal

This gear, although mounted with the sprocket, incorporates a friction disc for damping any shock loads developed in the transmission. The kick-starter assembles directly on to a spindle through the sprocket, the kick-starter pinion engaging directly with the main gear group.

The engine can be completely dismantled without taking it out of the frame. The silencer should be released first by undoing the two nuts holding the silencer bracket and the single nut holding the tailpipe bracket, all on the crankcase cover. The right-hand footboard can then be removed (as described in "Decarbonizing"). It is much easier to reach the appropriate screws to release the footboard if the silencer is removed first.

The kick-starter pedal arm can now be taken off by slackening the two pinchbolts, removing the circlip and the nut on the return-spring pin. As the pedal arm is eased off, a screwdriver should be laid under the spindle bearing down against the return-spring stud so that the spring tension can be eased off gradually. When the spring has unwound (about half a turn), the cover plate complete with spring can be taken off after the circlip is removed. If necessary a screwdriver can be inserted through the hole near the centre of the cover to lever the spring up to come away with the cover.

The crankcase cover is removed by unscrewing the 13 nuts which secure it to the crankcase, exerting gentle pressure on the clutch lever at the front

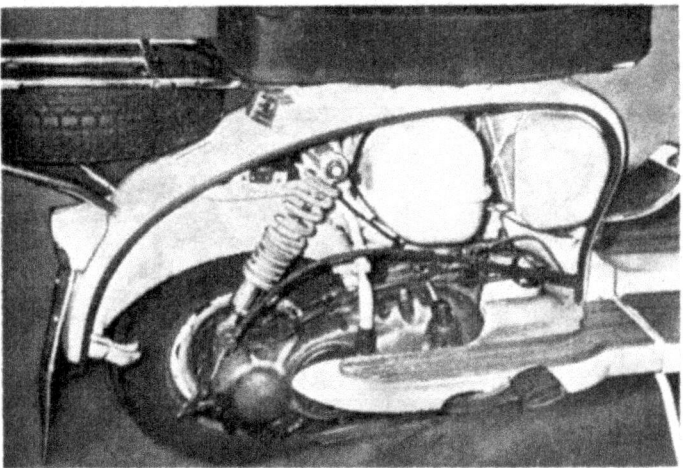

FIG. 25. VIEW OF ENGINE GROUP TV 175 SERIES I

The kick-starter is forward of the position occupied on Li and Series II machines and the crankcase is a different unit. Clutch is at the forward end.

of the cover, if necessary. Handle with care so as not to damage the gasket. Oil should, of course, be drained off from the crankcase first. The chain drive with its sprocket and pinion is now exposed and must be removed for access to either the clutch or gearbox. To do this it is only necessary to remove the circlip on the kick-starter spindle holding the friction damper and unscrew the seven bolts holding the engine sprocket housing and carrier assembly. The whole chain-drive assembly can then be lifted off complete. If stiff, two 14 mm bolts inserted in the threaded holes in the carrier plate can be used to extract the assembly. Particular points to note are the spacing washers behind the chain wheel used to give correct alignment (which must be replaced exactly as before); and the ball-bearing on the engine sprocket shaft which is now free and can fall out.

CHAIN DRIVE

The Duplex chain is pre-stretched and no adjustment of tension is provided, nor should it be necessary. Alignment of the chain is, however, extremely important and dependent on the original spacing washers being replaced exactly as before. If the engine is completely dismantled and reassembled, however, chain alignment would require checking with a special tool incorporating a dial gauge (Lambretta tool No. 57865). Chain alignment may also be affected if the torque damper is replaced or readjusted.

The damper operates on a similar principle to a clutch, being set to slip at a predetermined load (116 lb-ft torque). It can only be set accurately by a torque spanner applied to the ring nut. Its purpose is to slip if a sudden excessive load is applied to the transmission, as in a bad gear change, but to lock under all normal transmission loads. The only reason for departure from the original setting is to increase the slip load to 125 lb-ft for sidecar work, which is the only modification required to the Tv 175 (Series I) to adapt it for sidecar use. Actually this modification is only necessary if excessive slip is apparent when the machine is used for sidecar work.

Replacement of the chainwheel assembly calls for care, particularly in finding the correct alignment of the chain sprocket to align with the splined clutch centre, and also to avoid trapping the clutch plates when the carrier plate is screwed back in position. Lack of clearance between the short stub on which the clutch lever presses and the end of the sprocket shaft means that the clutch plates have been trapped and forced back in screwing the carrier home.

Care must also be taken when replacing the crankcase cover to see that the splines on the kick-starter spindle do not damage the oil seal. It is recommended that a metal thimble be placed over the end of the spindle to protect the oil seal, this being available as a special tool.

Before the kick-starter crank can be replaced it is necessary to tension the return spring correctly. The inner end of the spring is located in one of the three slots in the crankcase and a screwdriver (or a pair of screwdrivers) is used to wind the spring through one-half to two-thirds of a turn, not more. If the return-spring action is not sufficient with this spring tension then the fault lies elsewhere, e.g. the chain is too tight, the kick-starter bush too tight or the transmission stiff somewhere. Applying more spring pressure will only result in early failure of the spring.

CLUTCH

The clutch is fully exposed with the removal of the chain-drive assembly, as previously described. To dismantle the clutch a compressor (special tool) bolts on to the side of the crankcase and screws against the pressure plate so that the circlip can be removed. The compressor is then removed when the clutch discs, springs and cups can be removed. During

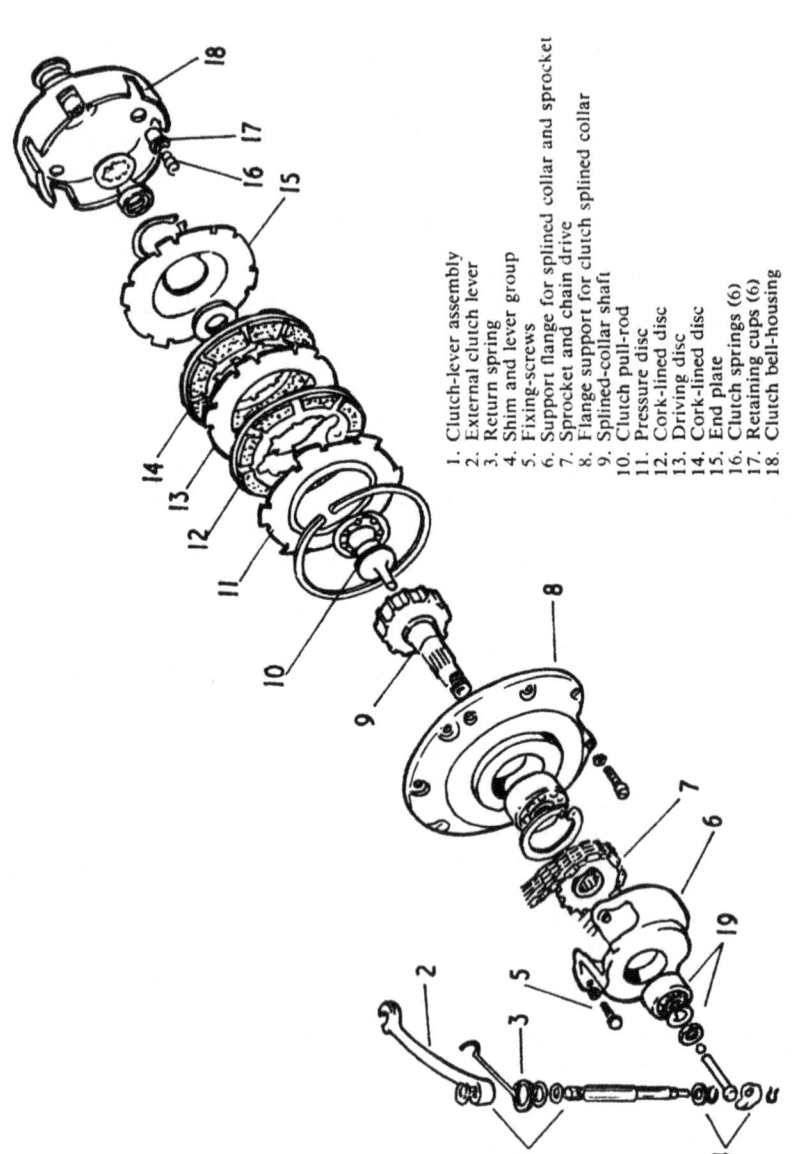

1. Clutch-lever assembly
2. External clutch lever
3. Return spring
4. Shim and lever group
5. Fixing-screws
6. Support flange for splined collar and sprocket
7. Sprocket and chain drive
8. Flange support for clutch splined collar
9. Splined-collar shaft
10. Clutch pull-rod
11. Pressure disc
12. Cork-lined disc
13. Driving disc
14. Cork-lined disc
15. End plate
16. Clutch springs (6)
17. Retaining cups (6)
18. Clutch bell-housing

FIG. 26. TV 175 SERIES I CLUTCH IN DETAIL.

reassembly the same special tool embodies an alignment piece which positions the plates so that when the circlip is finally back in position and the centre of the tool is removed, the clutch-plate splines are located ready to receive the splined centre of the engine sprocket group.

GEARBOX

With the crankcase cover and chain-drive assembly removed, the gearbox remains enclosed behind a flanged housing. This is held in place by five nuts which, when removed, allow the housing to be extracted with two 14 mm bolts screwed into the two threaded holes in the casting. The unit should come away together with the main gear-cluster shaft and its gear. The kick-starter spindle can also be withdrawn at this stage. The kick-starter pinion can be removed by extracting the circlip.

Before removing the rear wheel, the back of the crankcase should be properly supported. The centre wheel nut is then removed (on some models locked with an 8 mm left-hand thread screw; on others the nut may be locked by a serrated washer or spring washer). The wheel can then be withdrawn from the shaft by knocking sideways with a mallet on the tyre (or using an extractor tool, if available).

To remove the axle the tab washer must be bent back and the 36 mm nut holding the axle in its bearings removed, using a special tool to hold the shaft against rotation. The end of the shaft should then be tapped lightly with a mallet to free it from its bearing, when it can be withdrawn carrying the selector and gears, and also bringing with it the layshaft gear cluster. The arrangement of the gear groups can be identified from Fig. 27. The shaft gears can be slid or prised off after removing the two circlips and the roller-race ring similarly removed (preferably using the special tool mounted on the axle and with the handle of the tool secured in a vice). The two springs and ball-bearings which form the gear-engagement positions must be captured as soon as they are released by movement of the race ring.

Reassembly of the gears follows the reverse order, although there are several points to watch. Top gear and third gear must always be replaced with the lubrication grooves facing the outside of the crankcase. Second gear has no grooves but its boss must face the inside of the crankcase. First gear has lubrication grooves on both faces and must be replaced with the higher part of its boss facing the inside of the crankcase. If the gears are replaced incorrectly, the gearbox will seize in operation. If in doubt, make a note of the correct assembly at the time the gears are dismantled. Alternatively, place the disassembled gears together so that the gaps between all the dogs are equal, this indicating the correct order of reassembly.

After the axle and gear clusters have been reassembled it is important that the projection on the friction spring associated with the kick-starter ratchet is fitted into the recess in the crankcase and that there is a small

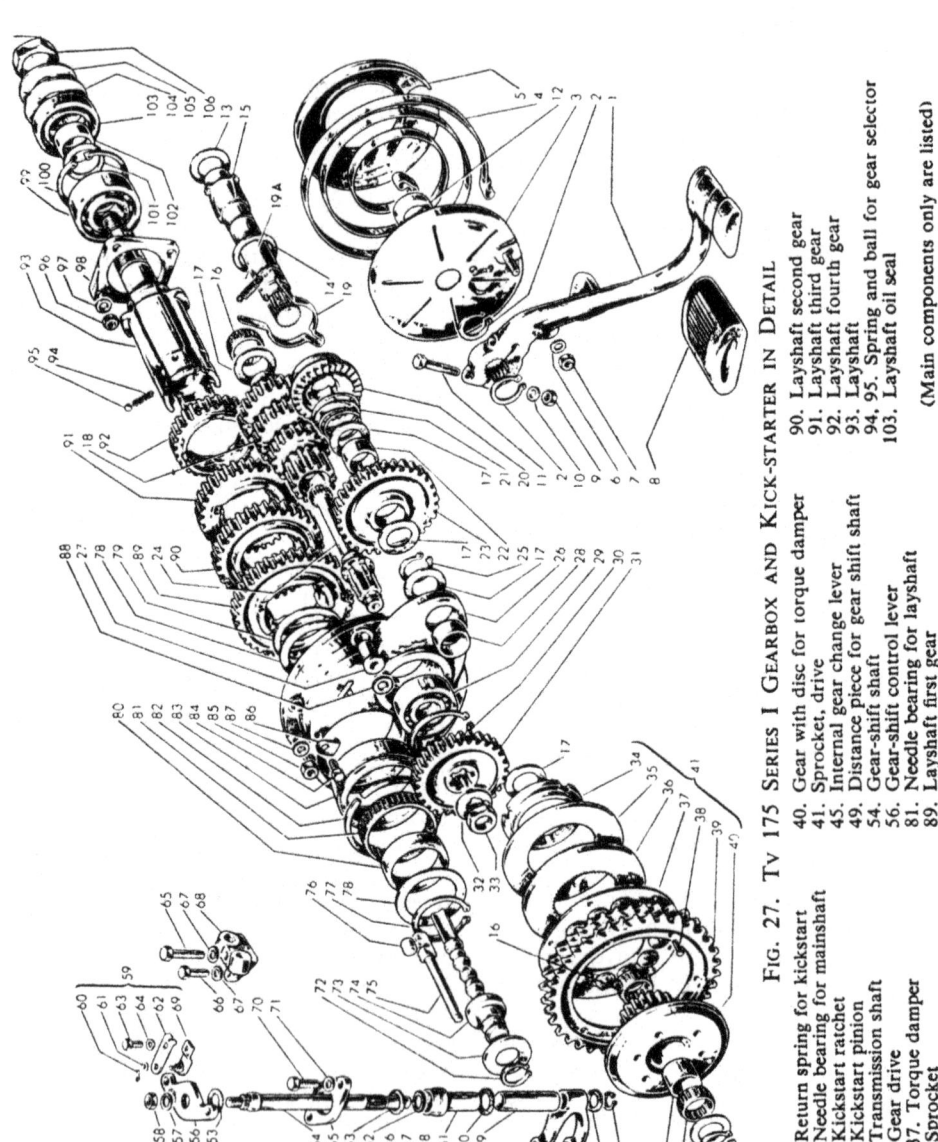

FIG. 27. TV 175 SERIES I GEARBOX AND KICK-STARTER IN DETAIL

4. Return spring for kickstart
16. Needle bearing for mainshaft
20. Kickstart ratchet
23. Kickstart pinion
24. Transmission shaft
31. Gear drive
34–37. Torque damper
39. Sprocket

40. Gear with disc for torque damper
41. Sprocket, drive
45. Internal gear change lever
49. Distance piece for gear shift shaft
54. Gear-shift shaft
56. Gear-shift control lever
81. Needle bearing for layshaft
89. Layshaft first gear

90. Layshaft second gear
91. Layshaft third gear
92. Layshaft fourth gear
93. Layshaft
94, 95. Spring and ball for gear selector
103. Layshaft oil seal

(Main components only are listed)

amount of end-float possible on the kick-starter spindle when the flanged housing is finally fitted.

CYLINDER UNIT

To gain access to the cylinder, remove the spark plug and then the engine cowl (held by two screws). The cylinder-head nuts can then be reached with a 12 mm box-spanner and the head withdrawn. After the induction manifold is removed, the cylinder can be withdrawn, exposing the piston. Note that there are gaskets under the head and under the cylinder, which must be replaced correctly during reassembly.

The gudgeon pin is retained by a circlip at each end and is a light push-fit so that it can readily be pushed out.

In the case of replacement parts, pistons and cylinders are matched according to three graded sizes (+, 0 or −) and so marked on the top of the cylinder and the crown of the piston. Both components must be marked with the same grading (*see* Appendix).

The piston is also marked with an arrow which must point towards the exhaust port on reassembly with the piston-ring pins facing the inlet port. If wrongly assembled, i.e. the pins facing the exhaust port, the piston rings will be trapped in the port and broken. Otherwise reassembly is straightforward, except that the ends of the piston rings may tend to open out into the inlet port and not let the cylinder be slid on properly. In such cases it is usually possible to close the rings sufficiently by inserting a screwdriver through the port to allow the cylinder to slide home.

CRANKCASE UNIT

To remove the crankshaft unit the clutch must be further dismantled on the right-hand side by undoing the 27 mm left-hand nut in the centre of the clutch bell, after first straightening out the tab washer. The crankshaft must be prevented from turning as this nut is unscrewed. The clutch bell can then be withdrawn from the crankshaft splines.

On the left-hand side the footrest must be removed, then the engine cowling and flywheel fan cover held by three screws to the magneto flange. The dust cover on the centre of the flywheel is then removed by taking off the retaining circlip. The central 19 mm nut is then exposed and after this is removed the flywheel can be drawn off with an extractor. The second half of the fan cover can now be detached.

The stator plate is held by five screws. Before it is removed its exact position should be marked, relative to the housing, so that it can be replaced correctly without upsetting the timing (*see* also Chapter 9). The flywheel support flange is fixed to the crankcase with six screws and, once these are removed, the flange can be withdrawn with an extractor. If the main bearing on the flywheel side is to be removed, release the circlip, slide off the oil seal, remove the circlip underneath and the thrust washer.

Three screws hold the bearing flange and, once these are removed, the bearing can be withdrawn with an extractor. On engines up to 5001 this bearing is a double-row ball-race, but on subsequent models is a roller-race.

The crankshaft can be removed from the crankcase with the engine dismantled to the above stage by tapping on the clutch side with a mallet.

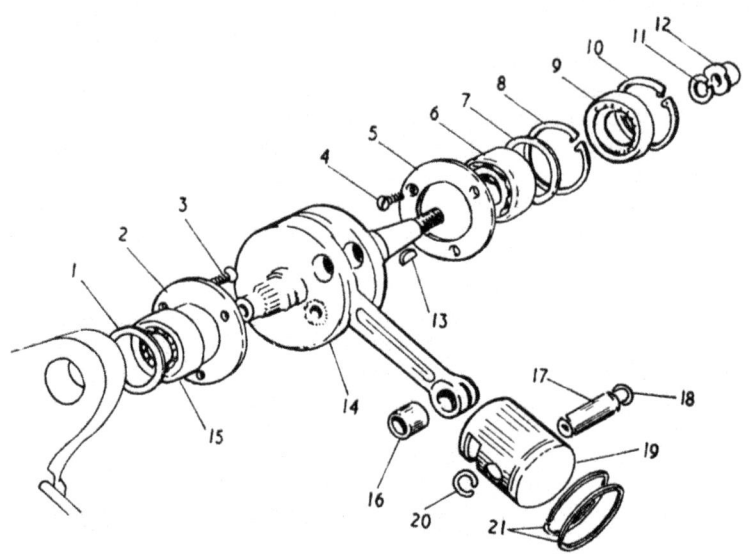

FIG. 28. CRANKSHAFT AND PISTON ASSEMBLY, TV 175 SERIES I

1. Thrust washer, drive side-bearing
2. Fixing flange
3. Flange locking-drive side-bearing screws (6)
4. Screws (6) fixing flange
5. Flange locking-drive side-bearing
6. Ball-bearing, flywheel side
7. Thrust washer
8. Circlip
9. Oil-seal, flywheel side
10. Circlip
11. Spring washer
12. Nut, locking flywheel to crankshaft
13. Woodruff key
14. Crankshaft assembly
15. Ball-bearing, drive side
16. Small-end bush
17. Gudgeon pin
18. Circlip
19. Piston
20. Circlip
21. Piston rings (2)

If necessary the complete crankcase can be removed from the frame after disassembling the engine and gearbox units, first removing the gear-change cable adjustment support and the clutch cable from its trunnion. Unscrew the 27 mm nut mounting the crankcase on its Silentbloc after opening out the tab washer and withdrawing the split-pin locking this nut in place.

Reassembly follows the reverse order, Fig. 28 providing reference. Make sure that all shims, etc. are replaced in exactly the same position as originally fitted. If the double-row ball-race on engines prior to No. 5001 is replaced with a roller-race, the additional clearance produced must be taken up by a 0·040 in. thick washer, if the original crankshaft is retained. A generous play in the bearings (in the region of 0·004 in.) is correct.

TV 175 SERIES I. SUMMARY OF STANDARD WORKSHOP OPERATIONS

The following summarizes briefly the sequence of operations for complete dismantling, as specified by Lambretta for workshop reference. Operations 1–40 cover dismantling the engine complete; operations 41–52 the handlebar group and control cables; operations 53–59 the tank: and operations 60–70 the front suspension—

SEQUENCE	OPERATION
1.	Remove side panels.
2.	Remove silencer.
3.	Remove right-hand footboard.
4.	Remove kick-starter pedal.
5.	Detach pedal return-spring cover.
6.	Drain crankcase.
7.	Free clutch cable.
8.	Free rear-brake cable.
9.	Remove rear-brake lever.
10.	Remove shock-absorber bolt.
11.	Remove gear-change control lever.
12.	Remove crankcase cover.
13.	Remove clutch flange and torque damper.
14.	Dismantle clutch.
15.	Remove gear-shaft support flange.
16.	Remove kick-starter pinion.
17.	Remove rear wheel.
18.	Remove axle-shaft.
19.	Remove axle-shaft gears.
20.	Remove carburettor and filter.
21.	Remove left-hand footboard.
22.	Remove spark plug.
23.	Remove engine cowl.
24.	Remove cylinder head.
25.	Remove carburettor induction manifold.
26.	Remove cylinder.
27.	Detach piston from connecting rod.
28.	Remove cowl cover.
29.	Remove dust cover.
30.	Unscrew flywheel nut.
31.	Remove flywheel.
32.	Remove flywheel cowl and flange.
33.	Disconnect wires from junction box.

SEQUENCE	OPERATION
34.	Remove stator plate.
35.	Remove flywheel support flange.
36.	Remove flywheel side main bearing.
37.	Remove clutch bell-housing lock nut.
38.	Remove clutch bell-housing.
39.	Remove crankshaft.
40.	Detach crankcase from frame.
41.	Unscrew handlebar-fairing fixing screws.
42.	Lift fairing and free speedometer.
43.	Pull out inner cable(s) to be replaced, insert new.
44.	Remove headlamp.
45.	Remove headlamp casing and front mudguard.
46.	Slide out cable outers (to replace complete cables).
47.	Remove clutch (or brake) lever point.
48.	Withdraw control shaft.
49.	Dismantle main switch (for fault on switch).
50.	Remove handlebars.
51.	Remove front fork.
52.	Align handlebars as necessary.
53–59.	Stages in removal of tank.
60.	Disconnect front brake at wheel, also speedometer cable.
61.	Remove front wheel.
62.	Remove shock absorber.
63.	Remove pivot pin on trailing link.
64.	Remove lower buffer.
65.	Remove trailing links.
66.	Remove pistons, etc.
67.	Unscrew wheel nut and withdraw left-hand distance piece.
68.	Withdraw front-wheel spindle.
69.	Remove oil seals on each side of hub.
70.	Remove bearings (right-hand bearing to the right; left-hand bearing to the left).

TV 175 SERIES I

The following refer to standard workshop operations as summarized in the schedule. Details of the individual operations can be found in the chapter, although not necessarily in the same order. The summary of operations must also be interpreted logically rather than literally, i.e. certain operations mentioned may not have to be fully completed. Reassembly follows in reverse sequence.

Part to be Replaced	Operations Required
Clutch discs	1–14
Piston	1, 2, 3, 8, 10, 20 and 27
Crankshaft	1–14, 20, 39
Crankshaft-drive oil seal . . .	1–14, 37 and 38
Crankshaft flywheel side oil seal .	1, 20, 21, 28–36
Gear-change ball-bearings . .	1, 13, 15, 17, 18, 19
Torque damper	1–13
Clutch spring on kick-starter . .	1–16
Rear-wheel shaft oil seal . . .	1, 17, 18
Front-wheel bearing . . .	60, 61, 67, 68, 69, 70
Front-suspension springs . .	60–6
Front fork	41, 42, 51, 61–6
Front mudguard	44, 45
Speedometer cable	41, 42, 44, 45
Rear-suspension unit . . .	1, 8, 10

Note—Procedure is similar for later models.

7 Engine Group Li
and Series I, II and III Models

Basic layout of the engine group on the Li and Series II Tv 175 models is shown in Fig. 29. The arrangement differs considerably from the Series I Tv, the clutch being mounted on the main gear group at the rear, dispensing with one gear set, and the kick-starter mechanism mounted

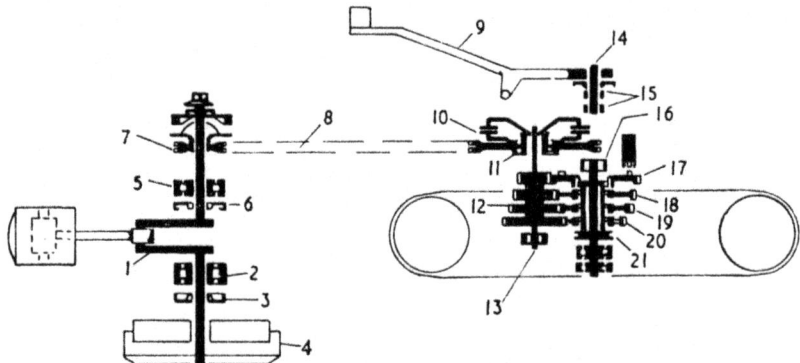

FIG. 29. ENGINE GROUP LI SERIES I AND ALL SERIES II AND III MODELS

1. Crankshaft
2. Ball-bearing main flywheel side
3. Oil-seal
4. Flywheel magneto
5. Ball-bearing, clutch side
6. Oil seal
7. Pinion and shock damper
8. Duplex chain drive
9. Kick-starter pedal arm
10. Clutch
11. Needle-bearing on clutch pinion

12. Main gear group
13. Needle roller-bearing
14. Kick-starter pinion
15. Bush for kick-starter pinion
16. Needle-bearing on layshaft
17. Layshaft first gear
18. Layshaft second gear
19. Layshaft third gear
20. Layshaft fourth gear
21. Layshaft

entirely in the crankcase cover. The primary drive is by Duplex chain from a pinion on the engine crankshaft, shock dampers being incorporated both at the pinion and sprocket ends of the drive. The following descriptions apply specifically to the Li Series I models. All Series II models are, however, essentially similar and in most respects identical. This applies also to the Series II Tv 175 which adopts common parts with the Li Series II models throughout, except where differences are obviously called for, e.g. piston cylinder and connecting-rod and gearbox gear ratios. Series III models are again similar but all employ a modified head design with higher compression ratio.

Access to the clutch, gearbox and engine is quite straightforward and work can be carried out on these components without removing the engine from the frame. Removal of the silencer, right-hand foot-board and freeing the clutch cable from the external lever on the crankcase cover enables the cover to be taken off, fully exposing the primary drive. The silencer is held by three nuts fixing it to the crankcase and is freed from the exhaust tube by slackening the clip (it may also be bonded lightly to the exhaust pipe with metallic sealer, particularly if the machine has been decarbonized at a service station at any time). The footboard is held by two nuts securing it to the frame. These are removed together with the screw fixing the frame connecting-piece and the two screws holding the footboard bracket.

Drain all the oil from the crankcase by removing the drain plug. The cover can then be taken off, once the thirteen nuts (spring washers under) are moved. The cover comes away complete with the kick-starter mechanism. The gasket should be treated carefully and not damaged; otherwise it will have to be replaced on reassembly. Further work on the various parts of the engine group is then best described under separate headings.

CLUTCH

A compressor tool is essential when dismantling the clutch. This is fitted to four of the crankcase studs, bridging the clutch. When the central part is screwed in, this bears against the clutch centre to compress the springs and enables the circlip to be removed with pliers. The tool is then removed when the clutch discs and springs can be taken out.

The inner clutch bell-housing is held by a 22 mm nut on the input gear main shaft, this assembly also being splined. It is necessary to hold the centre against rotation as this nut is removed, when the inner bell can be withdrawn outwards off the splines. This leaves the outer clutch member free, when it can be slid off the needle-roller races and removed by disengaging from the chain. It is particularly important that the distance washers between the clutch unit and the gearshaft bearing are collected and replaced as originally fitted, since these determine the chain alignment. Provided the sprocket is reassembled with these distance washers as before, no check on chain alignment should be necessary. If the chain sprockets are changed, however, or other work is carried out which could affect chain alignment, then it is strictly necessary to check the final alignment with a special bridge-piece and dial gauge (see Chapter 8).

Reassembly of the clutch should be quite straightforward, although holding the five springs in their sockets whilst the carrier plate is entered on to the splines of the clutch centre can be tricky. The compressor tool is applied again to compress the springs so that the circlip can finally be fitted. The freedom of movement of the plates on their splines should always be checked with the outer pressure plate in position as, otherwise, there is a possibility of distorting the centre piece.

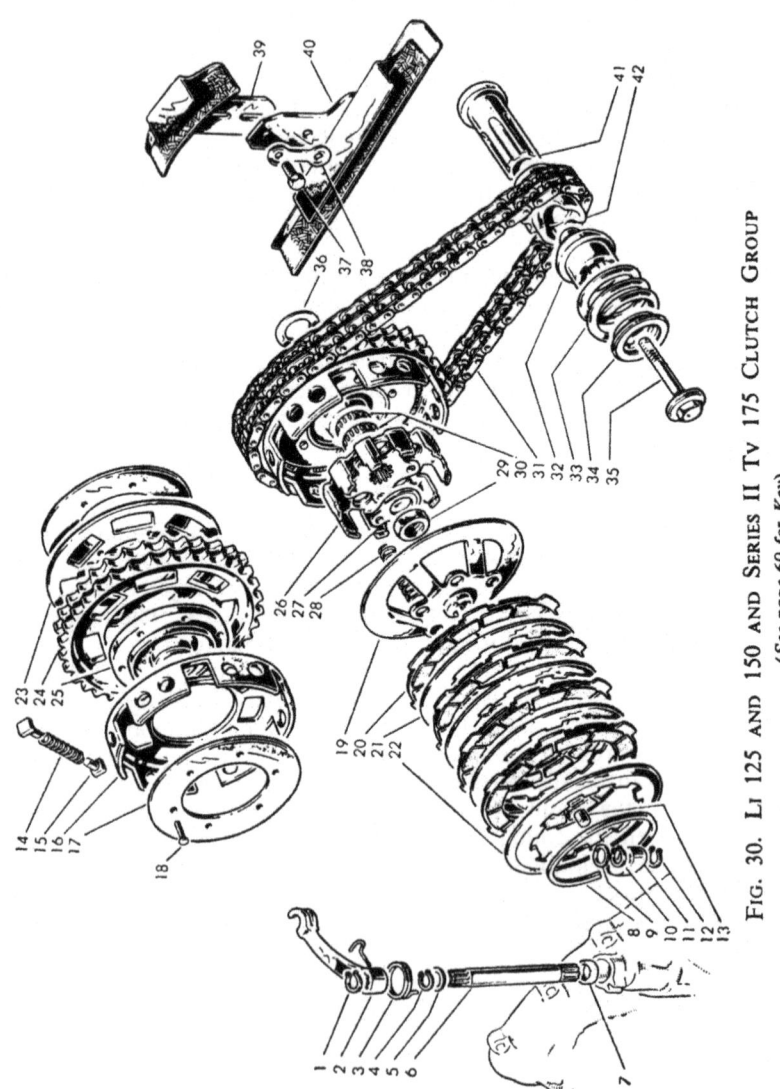

Fig. 30. Li 125 and 150 and Series II Tv 175 Clutch Group

(See page 69 for Key)

CHAIN DRIVE

The rear end of the chain is freed by dismantling the clutch, as described above. The chain run is provided with guides which are of a rubberized material. These should not normally need any attention although the upper guide is adjustable. It is held by the bolts in the slotted holes, and if these are slackened the guide can be moved. Primarily this adjustment is called for only during initial assembly of the machine to accommodate slight differences in individual engines. It should not need readjustment. If this adjustment is made, then the chain must never be tight. The chain is readily removed by detaching the guides complete (held by two screws).

KICK-STARTER

The kick-starter mechanism is retained within the crankcase cover. A return buffer in the form of a rubber bush is fitted into a lug on the cover and, as the pedal approaches this position, the ratchet is disengaged by an adjustable ramp secured to the inside of the cover.

The kick-starter shaft may be removed by holding the cover securely (e.g. in a vice), rotating the pedal arm to the end of its stroke and removing the cam. Then remove the pedal circlip and fixing bolt. Withdraw the pedal arm sufficiently for it to rotate freely clear of the buffer but do not remove at this stage. Use the movement of the pedal arm to free the spring; then the pedal circlip and washer can be removed, followed by the pedal shaft and spring.

The kick-start action piston can be removed by placing the shaft in a vice, unscrewing the peg and removing the circlip, disc, spring and pin, in that order.

Reassembly follows the reverse order. The pin is assembled first on the

---

(Key to Fig 30)

1. Circlip, for clutch lever	23. Disc, holding sprocket
2. Lever, external, clutch control	24. Sprocket
3. Return spring, for clutch external lever	25. Hub, for torque damper
4. Circlip, for clutch lever control shaft	26. Clutch bell, internal, with hub
5. Shim, for clutch control shaft	27. Thrust washer
6. Shaft, for clutch lever	28. Spring, for clutch discs
7. Seal ring, lower, for clutch lever shaft	29. Nut, for locking main gear group
8. Circlip ring, for clutch bell pressure discs	30. Bearing needle, for clutch bell
9. Shim, for clutch lever shaft	31. Chain, transmission
10. Ring, for internal clutch lever	32. Sliding dog
11. Lever, internal, clutch control	33. Spring
12. Circlip, for internal clutch lever	34. Washer, for spring
13. Push rod, clutch control	35. Screw, locking sleeve damper on crankshaft
14. Spring, for torque damper	36. Shim
15. End cap, for spring	37. Screw, fixing chain guide
16. Housing, clutch bell	38. Thrust plate
17. Driven disc, for torque damper	39. Chain guide, sliding
18. Rivet, for fixing torque damper disc	40. Chain guide, stationary
19. Flange, retaining springs with rods	41. Sleeve
20. Driving disc, cork lined	42. Sprocket, for chain
21. Driven disc, intermediate, for clutch	
22. Driven disc, external, for clutch	

shaft (ensure that it moves freely). Movement is limited by the peg which, when screwed in, must be burred over with a sharp punch. Then refit the spring, disc and circlip, in that order.

Before refitting the kick-starter shaft, the thread should be covered with a protective thimble to prevent damage to the oilseal in the crankcase cover as the shaft is pushed back. The shaft is inserted and the pedal arm slid on to the shaft but not pushed right home, so that it has full freedom of movement from stop to cover. The return spring can then be loaded by

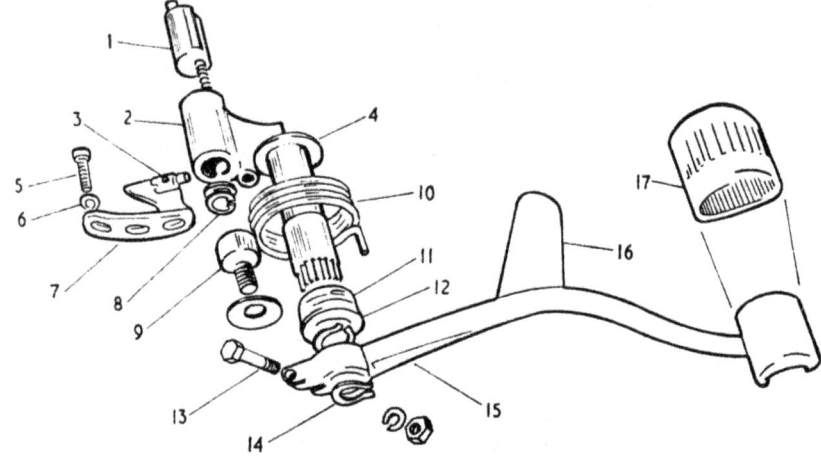

FIG. 31. KICK-STARTER ASSEMBLY

1. Piston for kick-start shaft	10. Return spring
2. Housing	11. Oil seal
3. Cam reference pin	12. Shim
4. Kick-start shaft	13. Pinchbolt
5. Screw fixing-cam	14. Circlip
6. Spring washer	15. Kick-starter pedal arm
7. Cam	16. Arm spur
8. Circlip for disc	17. Pedal rubber
9. Screw (stop for pedal arm)	

rotating the pedal arm until it comes up against the stop pin on the crankcase cover. With the pedal arm held in this position, the ramp should be fixed, but without tightening the three fixing-screws holding it to the inside of the cover.

The pedal arm is then released slowly and withdrawn. Refit completely home on the splines in such a position that, when it is up against its rubber buffer stop, the top of the tooth on the kick-start action pin is level with the kick-starter shaft and the body of the pin has no more movement than 1·5 mm (about $\frac{1}{16}$ in.) towards the inner end of the shaft. The ramp can be adjusted as necessary to arrive at this condition so that it withdraws the mechanism to the full extent of the ramp but allows plenty of clearance for further rotational movement of the shaft, with the result that the pedal buffer absorbs the return shock without imposing any load on the peg. If the pedal-arm position on the splines is not correct, or the ramp is incorrectly adjusted, premature engagement of the ratchet will result, indicated by noise when running. This fault must be cured since the ratchet teeth are being subjected to high wear under such conditions.

GEARBOX

The gearbox can be dismantled after removing the clutch, leaving the chain in place on the crankshaft sprocket. The gear-shaft support flange, uncovered by removal of the clutch, is held by six 11 mm nuts. These are removed and two 6 mm × 1 mm pitch screws inserted in the two threaded holes in the flange. As these are screwed in they will extract the flange, rotating the rear wheel, as necessary, to move the gears and allow the flange to come off complete with the input gear shaft and cluster.

The selector mechanism need not be dismantled unless the rear axle is to be taken out. In this case the arm is released by slackening the pinchbolt and sliding off the splines, noting particularly its original position. It must be replaced in exactly the same position on the splines, otherwise the position of the gear-change lever will not correspond with the gear engaged.

Before removing the rear wheel, the back of the crankcase should be properly supported. After removing the centre 27 mm nut the wheel can be knocked off by tapping the off-side of the tyre with a mallet. The stub axle (layshaft) can be freed by removing the circlip holding the gear-change lever shaft, withdrawing this shaft and tapping out the axle with a mallet from the near-side. Considerable care should be taken when withdrawing the selector cursor-ring from the shaft, as the two balls and springs will tend to fly out. Also, the cursor-ring is easily damaged once dismantled.

The four gears on the axle and the gear cluster can be interchanged as a group between the Li 125 and Li 150, the Li 125 gear ratios being adopted for the Li 150 when used for sidecar work. In the case of the Series II and III machines, the same considerations apply.

If complete sets of pinions and clusters are changed it is possible to change any Li model set with another Li model set, to alter gear ratios available. This would not normally be advisable, except to change to a lower gear ratio throughout for running with a sidecar fitted. In that case the following changes are recommended by Lambretta—

Li 150 to Li 125
SX 150 to GP 125
GP 150 to GP 125
SX 200 to Li 150
GT 200 to GP 125
TV 175 to Li 150

Gear Modifications. No gear modifications have taken place, the original ratios specified remaining standard on all models. The one exception is that of the Li 150 Special where a change was made to the third gear pinion form in later production models, the cluster being similarly modified to suit. If a third gear pinion has to be changed on this model, it is thus essential to change the whole cluster.

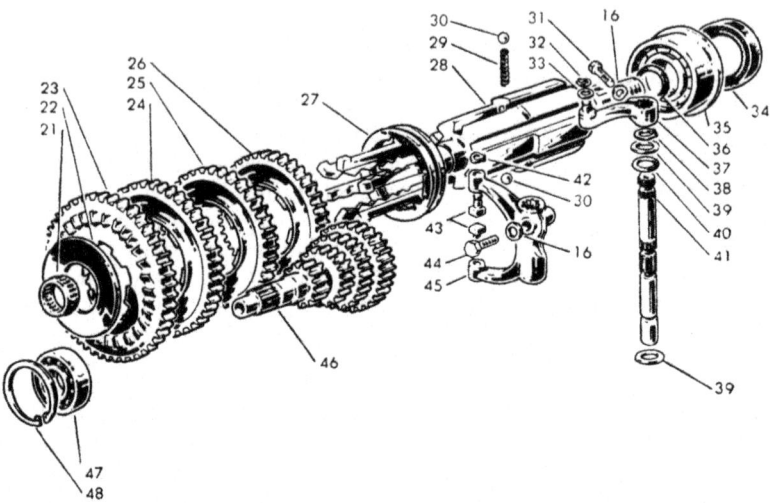

FIG. 32. GEARBOX UNIT (LI, ALL MODELS, AND SERIES II Tv)

16. Spring washer
21. Layshaft bearing needle
22. Shim
23. Layshaft first gear
24. Layshaft second gear
25. Layshaft third gear
26. Layshaft fourth gear
27. Sleeve with sliding dogs
28. Layshaft
29. Spring for balls
30. Ball for gear selector
31. Screw for external lever clamp
32. Circlip for gear control lever
33. Plain washer
34. Oil seal

35. Layshaft bearing
36. Seal ring on layshaft
37. External gearshift lever
38. Circlip
39. Thickness washer
40. Gasket
41. Gear shift shaft
42. Circlip for pins
43. Internal gear change lever pin
44. Locking screw
45. Internal gear change lever
46. Main gear group
47. Ball bearing for main gear group
48. Circlip

When reassembling the cursor-ring, the springs and two balls should be inserted first into the layshaft, the springs compressed by pressing on the balls and the ring slid on until it clicks into position. Particular care must be taken in reassembling the four gears on the axle, as they do not have the internal ring of dogs spaced centrally and thus each gear must be assembled the right way round to prevent jamming or malfunctioning. First gear, which is the largest gear, has dog teeth which are engaged by the kick-starter and so this side of the gear must face towards the outside of the crankcase (cover side). Second and third gears must have the high part of the boss facing the inside of the crankcase (wheel side). Fourth gear, the smallest gear, must have the high part of its boss facing the outside of the crankcase (cover side) so that the side with the dogs is facing towards the wheel hub when assembled. A simple check is to place all four gears together before assembly and check that the ring dogs and gear teeth are

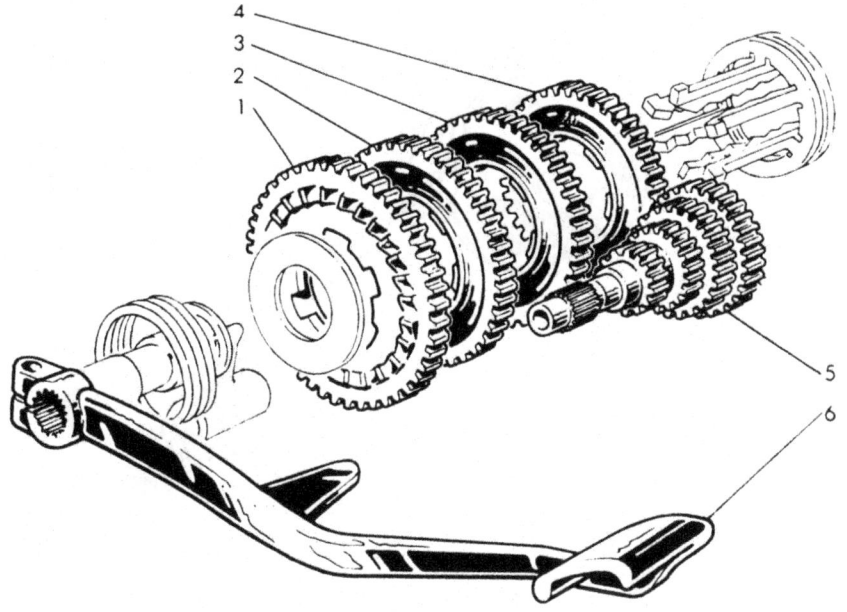

FIG. 33. GEARBOX 200 SX

1. First gear	3. Third gear	5. Mainshaft
2. Second gear	4. Fourth gear	6. Kickstart pedal

equidistant on all four gears. If the gaps are equally spaced, then the gears are grouped in the correct manner.

About the only other part to check is that, when the gear-shaft support flange is finally refitted, the two locating dowels fit correctly in their seatings.

The gearbox of the 200 SX is illustrated in Fig. 33.

PISTON AND CYLINDER

To gain access to the cylinder, the throttle cable should be disconnected from the carburettor and the clips securing the air intake to the frame and the carburettor to the manifold loosened. The carburettor and air intake can then be detached. Disconnect the choke control and fuel pipe. Take off the high-tension lead and remove the spark plug. The cylinder-head cowling is held by two screws on the fan cowl and one screw on the cylinder head. Once this cowl is detached, the four 14 mm head nuts can be removed with a box-spanner and the head and gasket withdrawn. The cylinder can follow, drawn off the studs, and also the cylinder gasket.

If the piston is to be removed, note that the gudgeon pin is held by circlips. Once these are removed, the gudgeon pin can be pushed out by

FIG. 34. PISTON GROUP 200 SX ENGINE
1. Crankshaft 2. Piston 3. Piston ring 4. Gudgeon pin 5. Washer

hand with a suitable drift. There should be no need to drive the gudgeon pin out forcibly.

Reassembly is straightforward, except that it is most important to replace the piston so that the arrow marked on the piston crown faces the exhaust port. In this position, the piston-ring stop pins also face the exhaust port. If fitted the other way round, the rings will inevitably be trapped in the port and cause serious damage.

Piston and cylinder must be correctly matched for size. There are three standard gradings, +, 0 and −, and the appropriate mark is carried on both the crown of the piston and the top of the cylinder. Only matched pairs can be used, i.e. piston and cylinder both bearing the same grading mark (*see* Appendix).

The piston group of the 200 SX is illustrated in Fig. 34.

SHOCK DAMPER

The shock damper is assembled with the crankshaft pinion on the chain-drive side. Its purpose is to provide a form of slipping-clutch action to prevent sudden overloads on the chain. To remove it, it is necessary to hold the crankshaft against rotation (e.g. by locking the connecting rod) when the 14 mm fixing-bolt in the centre can be unscrewed. Washer, spring, splined collar and sprocket then follow. Finally, the splined sleeve can be withdrawn with an extractor.

Reassembly follows the reverse order. To tighten the shock damper, the crankshaft must be rigidly held. Where the piston and cylinder have not been removed, a special tool can be employed to lock the inner clutch bell-housing and thus hold the damper sprocket via the chain. The damper fixing-bolt can then be screwed fully in.

CRANKSHAFT UNIT

The crankshaft can be removed without disturbing the clutch, first removing the shock damper complete on the chain side. On the opposite

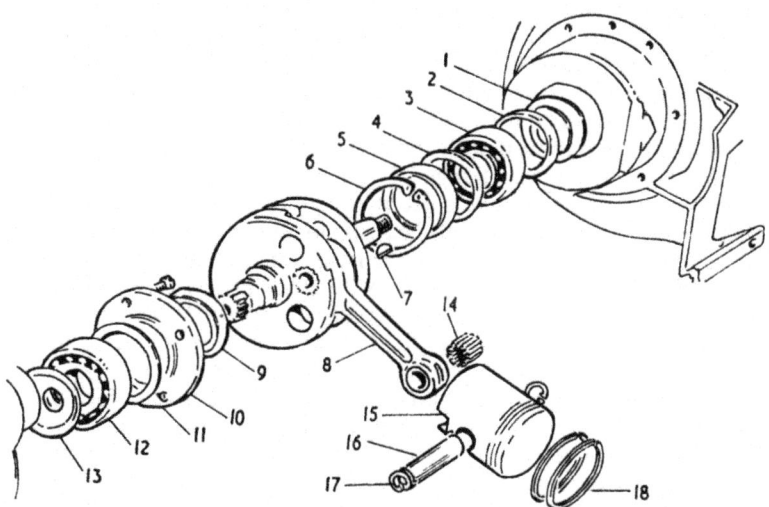

FIG. 35. CRANKSHAFT AND PISTON ASSEMBLY (LI, ALL MODELS AND SERIES II Tv)

1. Oil-seal, flywheel side
2. Retaining cup
3. Ball-bearing, flywheel side
4. Spacer
5. Oil seal
6. Circlip
7. Woodruff key
8. Crankshaft assembly
9. Oil-seal, drive side
10. Bearing flange
11. Thrust washer
12. Ball-bearing, drive side
13. Retaining cup for crankshaft bearing
14. Small-end bush or roller cage (according to model)
15. Piston
16. Gudgeon pin
17. Circlip
18. Piston rings

side of the engine, the fan-cover cowl is taken off by removing the five screws holding it in place, then the dust cover over the centre of the magneto unit. This cover may be held by a circlip or two screws, depending on the model. The flywheel can then be removed by unscrewing the 17 mm left-handed nut in the centre, holding the flywheel against rotation. Withdraw the flywheel by means of an extractor.

The stator plate is held to the flange by three screws. Before removing these and detaching the stator, mark the exact position of the stator relative to the flywheel housing, so that it can be reassembled exactly as before without altering the timing. Also disconnect the low-tension wiring from the socket. The stator plate will come away quite freely, exposing the magneto flange. This flange is held by three 10 mm nuts. Two of the stator-plate screws inserted into the threaded holes in the flange enable the flange to be extracted, being screwed in evenly to force the flange off. If the magneto flange is extremely tight a special tool may be required for extraction.

The crankshaft can now be tapped out from the crankcase end through the aperture uncovered by the removal of the magneto flange. It is important to use only a soft mallet or tap against something soft laid against the end of the shaft so as not to burr over the end.

If necessary, the crankshaft bearings can be removed. The main needle-roller race can be withdrawn with a special tool. The roller-bearing inner race can be removed with the crankshaft still in place, if preferred, after removing the magneto flange. The roller-bearing outer race, however, will prove difficult to remove since it is tightly fitted and this is really a workshop job. It is necessary to heat the magneto flange to about 150°C in oil to expand the housing and then tap out carefully. Extraction by driving out cold may cause damage to the housing. If the housing shows signs of scoring after the race is removed, the flange should be replaced. A new bearing must be shrunk-fitted in any case, heating the flange to about 150°C in oil, as above, to ensure uniform expansion.

The crankshaft roller-bearing inner race can be assembled with the crankshaft held in a vice by the flywheel side shoulder. The inner race is slid on to the cone of the shaft so that the higher side of the roller cage faces the crankshaft shoulder. The inner race is then lightly tapped into position, care being taken that it remains in perfect alignment with the shaft.

The ball-bearing on the crankshaft-drive side must be entered correctly into its seat and pushed fully home. It is then refitted from the inside of the crankcase together with its sealing ring and retaining flange. This race can only be extracted properly with a special tool.

The ball-bearing race on the drive side, combined with a roller race on the magneto side, gives an appreciable amount of sideways float and up-and-down movement on the flywheel side. Side-float may exceed 0·020 in. and still be quite normal and up to 0·003 in. big end play is permissible. This is a standard feature of the design and not a sign of wear or slack assembly.

If the crankcase is to be removed from the frame, the two screws holding the gear-change lever support, the two screws holding the clutch-adjuster support, and the rear-brake nut adjuster are removed. One of the nuts on the Silentbloc spindle can then be unscrewed allowing the spindle

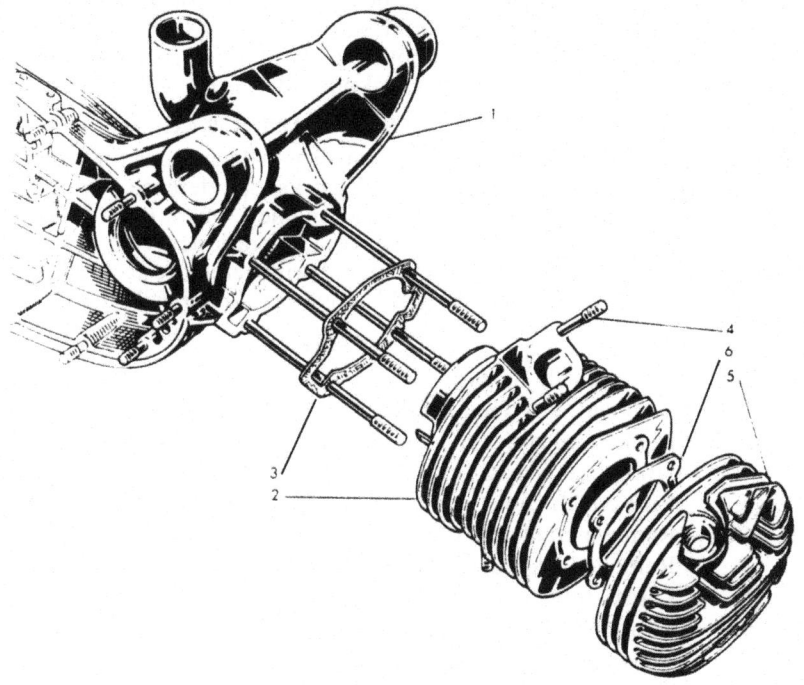

FIG. 36. CYLINDER-CRANKCASE OF 200 SX

| 1. Crankcase | 3. Gasket | 5. Cylinder head |
| 2. Cylinder | 4. Stud | 6. Gasket |

to be tapped sideways out of its seating and so free the crankcase casting. Other items to be dismantled to complete stripping down are the rear-brake cam, gear-change fork lever, rear-wheel stub axle bearings, rear-brake lever and cam, gear-selector lever and Silentblocs.

The cylinder-crankcase of the 200 SX model is illustrated in Fig. 36.

A considerable number of detail design changes have taken place through to and including the Li Series III models. This affects replacement parts since only new-type crankshaft assemblies are available from Lambretta as spares. These allow more side play to the big end bearing, and to centralize the connecting rod the piston bosses are machined to accept a shim on each side of the small end eye. When refitting a new-type crankshaft, a new-type piston is also required. However, a new-type piston can be used on an old-type crankshaft, simply by discarding the shims. New-type pistons are identified by a square stamped on the crown, together with an arrow or the letters SC (which must face towards the exhaust port when fitted).

New-type crankshafts are also specific to individual models, e.g. GT 200, SX 200, GP models and J range models. They are not interchangeable (although a GT 200 crankshaft could be used on a SX 200); and in the case of the GP models this also applies to the different engine sizes (the connecting rod, main bearing and crankpin differing).

LI MODELS SERIES I, 125 AND 150 c.c.

The following summarizes briefly the sequence of operations for complete dismantling, as specified by Lambretta for workshop reference. Operations 1–40 cover complete dismantling of the engine; operations 41–50 the handlebar group and control cables; and operations 57–65 the front suspension. Although specifically prepared with reference to the Series I Li models, the schedule generally holds good for all Series II models—

SEQUENCE	OPERATION
1.	Remove side panels.
2.	Remove right-hand footboard.
3.	Remove silencer.
4.	Drain crankcase.
5.	Free clutch cable.
6.	Remove crankcase cover.
7.	Remove kick-starter shaft.
8.	Disassemble kick-starter.
9.	Dismantle clutch plates.
10.	Unscrew inner bell nut.
11.	Remove inner and outer clutch bell-housing.
12.	Remove chain guides.
13.	Remove gear-shaft support flange.
14.	Withdraw gear shaft complete.
15.	Raise rear on to suitable stand.
16.	Remove rear wheel.
17.	Remove rear-wheel stub axle.
18.	Withdraw cursor-ring.
19.	Remove suspension unit.
20.	Remove crankcase engine return buffer and drop cylinder.
21.	Remove left-hand footboard.
22.	Remove carburettor and air intake.
23.	Detach high-tension lead and remove spark plug.

SEQUENCE	OPERATION
24.	Remove cylinder-head cowl.
25.	Remove cylinder head.
26.	Remove cylinder.
27.	Remove piston and gudgeon pin.
28.	Remove fan cowl cover.
29.	Remove dust cover.
30.	Remove flywheel.
31.	Remove stator plate.
32.	Remove flywheel support flange.
33.	Remove engine-sprocket shock damper.
34.	Remove crankshaft.
35.	Remove main shaft needle-roller outer race.
36.	Dismantle crankshaft bearing.
37.	Dismantle roller-race inner bearing.
38.	Remove roller-bearing outer race.
39.	Remove crankcase from frame.
40.	Complete dismantling of crankcase.
41.	Unscrew screws holding handlebar centre-fairing.
42.	Lift fairing and free speedometer.
43.	Pull out cable inners and replace, as necessary.
44.	Remove headlamp.
45.	Remove headlamp casting and front mudguard.
46.	Replace cable outers (or complete cables) as necessary.
47.	Remove throttle and gearshift control shafts.
48.	Remove handlebars.
49.	Remove front fork.
50.	Realign handlebars and front wheel.
51–6.	Remove fuel tank.
57.	Release front-brake cable and speedometer drive from front wheel and suspension box.
58.	Remove front wheel.
59.	Remove lower buffers.
60.	Remove trailing links.
61.	Remove pistons, etc.
62.	Unscrew right-hand wheel nut and withdraw brake backplate.
63.	Withdraw front-wheel spindle.
64.	Remove oil seals and distance pieces (each side of hub).
65.	Extract front-wheel bearings (right-hand bearings towards the right; left-hand bearing towards the left).

LI SERIES II MODELS

The following sequence of operations necessary for replacement of the parts specified refers to the workshop-schedule items. These should be interpreted logically rather than absolutely literally, referring to the main text for appropriate details. Reassembly follows the reverse sequence.

Replacement Part or Component	Operations Required
Clutch discs	1, 2, 3, 4, 5, 6, and 9
Piston	1, 2, 3, 15, 19, 20–7
Crankshaft	1, 2, 3, 4, 5, 6, 9, 10, 11, 12, 15–19, and 34
Small-end bush . . .	1, 2, 3, 15, 19, 20, 26, 27
Outer clutch bell-housing .	1, 2, 3, 4, 5, 6, 9, 10, 11
Selector cursor-ring . .	1, 2, 3, 4, 5, 6, 9–18
Crankshaft drive-side oil seal .	1, 2, 3, 4, 5, 6, 9, 10, 11, 12, 15, 17, 19–34
Crankshaft flywheel-side oil seal	1, 21, 22, 28, 29, 30, 31, 32
Rear stub-axle-bearing oil seal	1, 15, 16
Rear suspension . . .	1, 15, 19
Front fork	58, 59, 60, 61, 41–2, 48–9
Front mudguard . . .	44, 45
Front-suspension springs .	57, 58, 59, 60, 61
Front-wheel bearings . .	57, 58, 62, 63, 64, 65
Speedometer cable . .	41, 42, 44, 45

Note—Procedure is similar for later models.

CHANGES IN ENGINE PARTS

The following are the more important changes in the detail design of engines which can affect replacement parts. New parts, specifically produced for a later model, cannot always be used on an older model. In many cases, too, late model replacement parts only are available, which may call for additional parts to be used to complete a reassembly satisfactorily.

Parts	Models	Changes
CRANKSHAFTS	Li Series I and II	Replacement crankshafts will require matching new-type piston, new main bearings, new magneto flange and other miscellaneous parts.
	GT 200	New crankshaft has flats machined on the counterbalance.
	SX 200 . . .	New crankshaft also needs new piston, new gudgeon pin.
	GP models . .	No difficulty, but replacement crankshaft is specific to engine size.
	J range . . .	Latest (modified) crankshaft is identified by two small flats on the webs close to the crankpin.
	125 Starstream .	A completely individual design, not interchangeable with the J range.
CYLINDERS	Li Series I . .	Identified by only three fins below the exhaust port, also shorter. Require matching Series I piston.
	Li Series II and III .	Four fins below exhaust port. *Note:* 125 Li Series I cylinders are no longer available. A Series II cylinder can be used, with matching piston, new cowling and longer hold-down screws.
	150 Li Special .	Identified by two notches in top fin.
	SX 150 . . .	Two notches in top fin, slots on the base flange and smaller inlet port.
	SX 200 and GP 200	Two notches in the top fin.
	GT 200 . .	A number of modifications were made during the production run affecting the shape of the exhaust ports. Later types had deep and narrow ports.
PISTONS	Li Series I . .	Skirt cut away on either side to match transfer ports and also shorter than later models.

Parts	Models	Changes
PISTON RINGS	Li Series II . .	Longer piston with continuous skirt and transfer holes in walls.
	Li 150 Series III .	Transfer holes modified to slots (interchangeable with earlier Series III pistons).
	200 models . .	Transfer ports modified in shape. Piston ring peg positions changed.
	J range . . .	Pistons are gudgeon pins supplied as matched pairs (colour-coded either black or white).
	Li 125 and Li 150 .	2 mm thick rings were introduced at *circa* 1965–6. Spares are now of this size only.
	Tv 175 Series III .	Three 2 mm thick rings employed (differing from the two 2·5 mm thick rings on Series I and II). *Note:* piston ring peg positions have also changed (see above).
CYLINDER HEADS	SX 150 . . .	Two head gaskets fitted as standard.
	GP 150 . . .	One head gasket fitted as standard.
	SX 200 . . .	Early design of cylindrical head was changed to offset "squish" head on later models. Early heads use a 2 mm thick gasket; later heads a 1·5 mm thick gasket.
SILENCERS	Li 125 and 150, Series I and Series II	Early version had long silencer stub and short tail pipe; later version short stub and long tail pipe. These should not be regarded as interchangeable without modification of carburettor air intake.
	Li Series III (Slimstyle) .	Blank-ended cone baffle introduced.
	SX 150 and GT 200	Perforated baffle used. Replacement type for GT 200 has an additional bracket mounting requiring a blind hole (0·5 in.) to be drilled in the block cast in the underside of the crankcase and tapped to take a 6 mm bolt.
	J Range . .	Starstream silencer has an additional mounting bracket. It can be fitted to the J 125 with modification of crankcase, as above.

8 Further details

THE following descriptions apply to components and assemblies not covered in the chapters on the engine group or fully described under the general maintenance headings. They can be taken as applying to all Li and Tv models, except where noted otherwise. Detail differences may, however, exist as far as individual machines are concerned, as minor modifications and amendments to the basic design are numerous and continue to appear. In all cases when ordering spare parts, etc., it is therefore essential to quote the engine and chassis number so that the correct replacement part is obtained, even though this may appear as a nominal standard throughout the whole series.

CARBURETTOR

A Dell'Orto carburettor is standard on all models, type numbers being as under—

Li 125, Series I: MA 18 BS 5
Li 125, Series II: MA 18 BS 5 or
     MA 18 BS 7
Li 125, Series III: SH 1 18
Li 150, Series I: MA 19 BS 5
Li 150, Series II: MA 19 BS 5 or
     MA 19 BS 7
Li 150, Series III: SG 1 18
175 Tv, Series I and early Series II:
     MB 21 BS 5
175 Tv, Series II: MB 21 BS 7
175 Tv, Series III: SH 1 20

Li 150 Special: SH 1 18
150 SX: SH 1 20
125 DL: SH 1 20
150 GP: SH 2 22
200 Tv: SH 1 20
200 SX: SH 1 20
200 GP: SH 2 22
JI 25: SHB 18 16
JI 25 Starstream: SHB 18 16

The MA and MB types, fitted to earlier machines; and the SH and SHB types fitted to later models, differ both externally and internally. Component parts for MB carburettors are shown in Fig. 37, the MA being similar. The SH and SHB types are similar to each other, and the SH type is shown in Fig. 38. The SHB carburettor was fitted to J range models only.

Full details of jet sizes, etc., of all types are summarized in Table 9.

All carburettors are essentially similar and differ only in jet and needle sizes (see Table 9). Component parts are shown in Fig. 37, for which the following general comments apply.

The choke control is operated by a 180° movement of the choke knob on the right-hand side of the vertical body panelling in front of the saddle. This operates via a cable on the choke assembly which, effectively, acts as a separate carburettor pre-set to give a very rich mixture for starting when the engine is cold. It is most effective when the throttle is closed.

The main jet is located under the main mixing chamber of the carburettor with the needle immediately above it in the throttle slide. The needle has three notches and is normally located on the middle notch. With correct jet sizes, and undamaged jets and needle, it is a feature of all engines that they two-stroke readily under all operating conditions. However, in some cases, if even two-stroking is not obtained at normal cruising speeds, this fault may be cured by lowering the needle in the slide, i.e. locating it in the top groove.

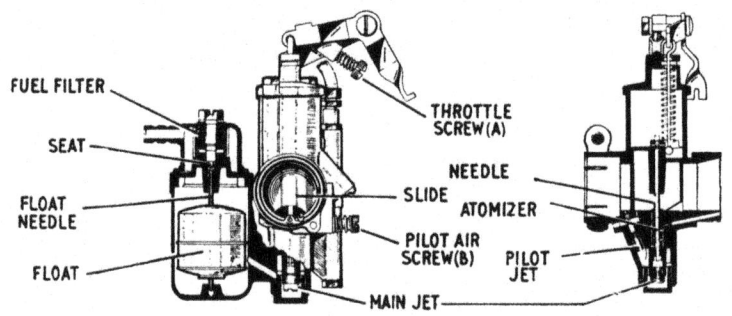

FIG. 37. DELL'ORTO CARBURETTOR ESSENTIALLY SIMILAR ON ALL SERIES I AND II MODELS

Slow-running adjustments must always be made after a run while the engine is still warm. Two screws are involved in this adjustment. one at the top of the carburettor, which controls the closed position of the slide and the other on the side, which controls the amount of air drawn in to mix with the fuel supplied from the slow-running jet. Screwing the throttle screw in will open the throttle, and vice-versa. Screwing the pilot air-screw in will enrich the slow-running mixture, and vice versa. The two must be adjusted together for best results, since the effects are interdependent.

Correct technique is to adjust the throttle screw until a rather fast idling speed is obtained. Screw B is then adjusted to give the smoothest possible running. Screwing in to enrich the mixture will increase the idling speed. Screwing out to weaken the mixture will reduce idling speed, eventually to a point where the engine will stop altogether.

It is, therefore, necessary to adjust the throttle and pilot air-screws alternatively to arrive at the best results. The usual position of the pilot air-screw for best results is three-quarters to one turn open. If satisfactory slow running is achieved but the engine tends to hesitate or misfire when the throttle is opened up, the pilot air-screw is too far out and must be screwed in a little and the slow running re-established.

The tapered needle controls the normal running mixture, and nearly always the middle-notch position will be correct. If, however, the mixture is obviously incorrect, indicated by reluctance to two-stroke with the

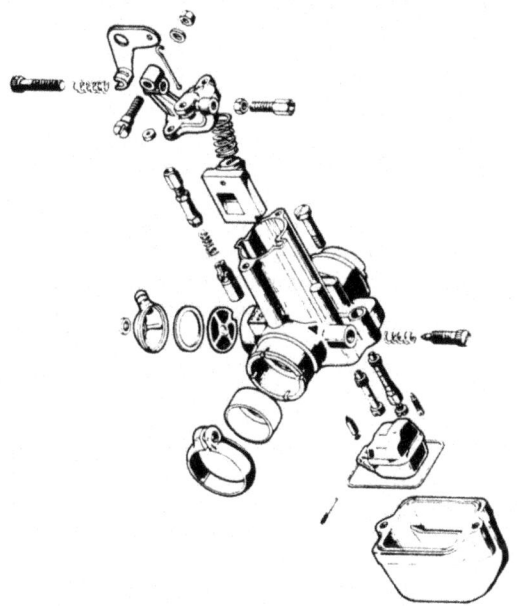

Fig. 38. SH 1 and SH 2 Carburettor

throttle open, the engine overheating or running badly (indicating a mixture which is too rich or too weak), one of the other notch positions on the needle may provide a cure. Unless the owner is familiar with carburettor behaviour, however, it would be best to have such a fault checked by a recognized service agent. Slow-running adjustment, on the other hand, is something that any owner can attempt satisfactorily, since this is merely a case of "trial and error" observation and no harm, only inconvenience, is likely to result from faulty settings.

A Dell'Orto SH 1 or SH 2 carburettor is fitted to all Series III machines and the GT 200. This carburettor differs in several details from the earlier models.

The original slide/needle mechanism is replaced by a flat slide which carries a recess on the inner side to permit an automatic air balance to both sides of the slide. The dimensions of this recess is calibrated to suit the cubic capacity of the particular machine involved and therefore should it be necessary for a replacement to be fitted, careful note should be made of the casting number impressed into the slide casting. The conical needle of the old type is therefore eliminated entirely.

The float assembly is seated in the float chamber directly over the venturi of the carburettor and not to one side as on the previous models. The shut-off valve mechanism is of the latest design, incorporating a Neophrene type of shut-off needle to ensure positive closing of the fuel entry, when the correct fuel level is reached.

The slow running and starter jets are independent from the main jet, all jets being housed within the float chamber compartment. When servicing is found necessary extreme care should be taken when removing and refitting jets, to ensure that the jets are replaced into their correct positions and not overtightened. When adjusting the slow running mixture control, this item is the only adjustable jet fitted to the carburettor. Care should be taken to avoid damaging the tip through overtightening. The general setting for this jet is approximately one turn out from the fully screwed home position.

Screwing in the jet weakens the mixture, but this adjustment has no influence whatsoever on the working of the main jet.

The opening and closing of the choke is similar to the old type, i.e. through the movement of the piston controlled by an external lever. It is advisable to ensure that when the choke is closed, the piston should be at the end of its stroke, allowing a small amount of free play on the control cable. When the choke is open, the piston should be raised between 5 and 6 mm.

For the perfect functioning of the new carburettor it is essential that the characteristics of the air intake, air filter, the exhaust manifold and the exhaust muffler are not altered in any way.

For correct performance from the carburettor it is important to see that it is fitted to the engine in such a manner that the float chamber is perfectly vertical, otherwise the float could stick and cause petrol to spill, as well as possibly upsetting the mixture. Both manifolds must also be tightly fitted to avoid air leaks which will seriously affect the mixture, but not excessively tightened, otherwise the plastic insulating gasket can be distorted.

Maintenance demands periodic cleaning, when the whole of the carburettor should be disassembled and jets blown through to clear and all holes and crevices in the carburettor body similarly blown out. Jets should *never* be cleaned by pushing a wire through them, as they are calibrated to exact size and these sizes are critical. The reaming action produced by forcing a wire through the hole can completely upset the performance of the carburettor. Blowing through to clear, or using compressed air, if available, is by far the most satisfactory method of cleaning. If there is a definite blockage which cannot be cleared by blowing, then a non-metallic bristle can be used to poke it clear.

Jets are unlikely to deteriorate through wear but the taper length of the needle may well show signs of wear after a considerable period of use. In this case it should be replaced. The condition of the atomizer into which the needle enters should also be examined and this replaced if it shows signs of wear.

The float needle should also be in perfect condition (and replaced, if suspect) and also its seating at the upper end. The float itself is unlikely to get damaged, but if it is, then this will show up at once as a carburation fault.

Dirt, grit, etc., is the main enemy of the carburettor; hence it is important to keep both the air filter and the petrol filter clean and free from deposits which they may collect. Neither should need replacement, provided they are checked and cleaned at intervals (the petrol filter periodically and the air filter regularly).

CHAIN ALIGNMENT

Where new sprockets are fitted, it is virtually essential to check the chain alignment after final assembly. A chain which is not aligned correctly will develop high wear, far more so in the case of the Duplex chain employed than a single chain, which can tolerate a small amount of misalignment.

To check chain alignment a special tool is used, incorporating a dial gauge. Procedures are slightly different for the Series I Tv 175 and for the other models.

In the case of the Series I Tv 175 the dial gauge has a 31 mm long, solid-pointed extension. The flywheel is locked, the tab washer straightened out and the nut holding the clutch splined collar removed with the shaft support and ball-bearing. The flywheel locking-tool is then removed and the chain pinion tapped to its farthest position nearest the clutch.

The spark plug is removed so that the engine can be turned over easily. The dial-gauge tool is then placed across the back of the chain by the larger sprocket and readings taken in at least three different rotational positions of the torque damper. If the difference between any two readings is greater than 0·15 mm (6 thou.) the torque damper must be replaced.

Measurements are now repeated at the front end of the chain, ensuring that the torque damper is dead against its collar by tapping in. Readings should be between 0·05 and 0·1 mm lower than the previous readings. If not, shims must be added behind, or taken away from behind, the torque damper until correct positioning is obtained.

Finally, the shims are replaced in front of the damper disc and retained with the circlip. The damper is pulled outwards as far as possible, when readings made on the dial gauge should be 0·05 to 0·1 mm higher than that made for the pinion. Again, if this is not obtained, adjust the number and thickness of shims on the outside of the damper, as necessary.

On other models, chain alignment is checked with a similar gauge after removing the shock-damper sprocket bolt together with its washer, spring and splined collar. The sprocket itself must remain tight against its splined sleeve. The dial gauge is then used to measure the distance to the sprocket face, bringing the dial gauge reading to zero. The gauge is then placed across the crankcase over the rear sprocket and the distance to the main sprocket of the rear axle measured. The difference between the two readings should be between *plus* 0·05 mm (2 thou.) and *minus* 0·25 mm (10 thou.).

If readings are not obtained within these limits, it will be necessary to dismantle both the clutch housings and increase or decrease the thickness of shims on the primary shaft between the inner bell-housing and the ball-bearing, as appropriate.

REAR-AXLE BEARING

The oil seal in the rear axle can be replaced simply by taking off the hub and removing the bearing retaining-plate and washer (held by four nuts). The oil seal can then be prised out with a suitable tool (e.g. a screwdriver).

If the bearing itself is to be changed, this can be done without dismantling the gearbox by simply taking off the crankcase cover, engaging top gear and gently tapping the axle towards the near-side. This will dislodge the bearing from its seating, but care must be taken not to drive the axle too far as otherwise the springs and balls governing the gear-change positions will be released and will fly out. When tapping the axle back into position it will be necessary to re-align first gear, which will have dropped down, and also to ensure that the washer is correctly positioned. A fair amount of play is standard on the rear-wheel bearing and this should not be misinterpreted as undue wear calling for a new bearing. When reassembled with a new bearing there will still be an appreciable clearance.

REAR HUB

The hub is of cast aluminium with cast-in iron brake liner and boss on all models, only in the case of the J range the sizes are different. The hub is held by a split taper cone, the splines on the shaft and cone merely locating the hub and preventing it moving when the nut is tightened.

It is important that the retaining nut be tightened to the correct torque, using a torque spanner. Tightening torques are 110–120 lb-ft for the Li Series; and 80 lb-ft for the J range.

Cone angles may be found to differ. On early models the angle was 20 degrees, but it was replaced by an 11 degree cone (replacement 20 degree cones no longer being available). The 11 degree cone was used up to the GP models, when the cone angle was changed again to 8 degrees. The latter can be identified by part numbers starting 1954.

REAR SUSPENSION

The rear-suspension unit is basically similar on all models and consists of a hydraulic shock-absorber surrounded by a coil spring. It is attached by two fixing nuts, one at each end, and when these nuts are removed the unit can be withdrawn complete by sliding the Silentbloc mounts off their respective pins on the frame and crankcase. If the rear-suspension unit proves to be difficult to remove by hand, each end can be gently drifted off from the wheel side.

FIG. 39. REAR-SUSPENSION ATTACHMENT POINTS
(SILENTBLOCS) ARROWED
Series I Tv and all Series II models utilize a double spring

On the Series I Li models the outer spring comprises a single spring assembled against a centring ring and half-ring and half-ring lock on the lower end of the shock-absorber body. On the Series I Tv 175, upper and lower springs are assembled on the shock-absorber, separated by a distance washer with a distance washer and half-ring lock at the lower end. On Series II machines this double-spring arrangement is used and the shock-absorber may be one of two types (Riv. or S.C.M.).

On Series III machines, an improved hydraulic shock-absorber of similar overall appearance is employed, with an identical method of fixing.

The performance of the suspension can only be judged by road test. No adjustment is possible and if it is felt that it is not satisfactory or could be improved, then the only solution is to fit a service exchange unit.

A new type of silent bloc engine mounting bush is fitted to all Series III models to reduce the transmission of engine vibration to the frame.

The engine mounting bolt has been lengthened and the bushes are wider with three holes. These bushes must be fitted with two holes facing forward and one downwards. They will not be effective if fitted in any other position. The GT 200 suspension is identical to that of the Series III models.

FRONT-WHEEL SHOCK-ABSORBER

A hydraulic shock-absorber is fitted to the front suspension on 175 c.c. and 200 c.c. models only. This is of the single-acting type which offers damping only when being extended. Thus, if removed, it will be found easy to compress the shock-absorber, although considerable resistance should be felt if it is extended rapidly. The shock-absorber will not work in an inverted position, or even when horizontal. These features are worth noting since it is easy to imagine that the unit is faulty when it can be operated freely without giving damping in such positions. It attaches to a lug on the front forks by means of a screw, spring washer and nut at the upper end; and by a nut and washer on a pin screwed into the trailing link at the lower end. Li Series front forks are not suitable for fitting a shock-absorber.

TABLE 9
CARBURETTOR DETAILS

	MA 18 BS 5	MA 19 BS 5	MA 18 BS 7	MA 19 BS 7	MB 23 BS 5	MB 21 BS 5	MB 21 BS 7	SH 1 18
Choke (mm)	18	19	19	19	23	21	18	18
Slide . .	50	65^3 or 50^4	50	50	70	70	70	5914 1 or 2
Needle .	$D16^1$ or $D20^2$	$D18^3$ or $D21^4$	D21	D21	E15	E15	E15	—
Atomizer .	260 OB	260 OB	260 B	260 B	260 B	260 B	260 B	5899 1 or 2
Main jet .	92^1 93 or 73^2	95^3 102 or 78^4	78	78	110	88	88	99^5 105^6 101^7
Pilot jet .	35	40	40	40	40	40	40	42^5 45^6 45^7
Starter jet .	55	55	55	55	60	55 or 60	60	50
Float (grams)	6·5	6·5	5	5	6·5	6·5	5	5
Air screw adjustment .	½–2 turns	½–2 turns	½–2 turns	½–2 turns	½–2 turns	½–2 turns	½–2 turns	½ turn
Fitted to .	^{1}Li 125 I ^{2}Li 125 II	^{3}Li 150 I ^{4}Li 150 II	Li 125 II (later models)	Li 150 II (later models)	175 Tv (early models)	175 Tv Series II	175 Tv Series II (later models)	^{5}Li125III ^{6}Li150III ^{7}Li 150 Special

TABLE 9 (contd.)

	SH 1 20	SH 1 20	SH 1 20	SH 1 20	SH 1 20	SH 2 22	SH 2 22	SHB 18/16
Choke (mm)	20	20	20	20	20	22	22	16
Slide	5914 2	5914 2	5914 1	5914 1	5914 1	7895 2	7895 1	6492 1
Needle	—	—	—	—	—	—	—	—
Atomizer	5899 5	5899 4	5899 2	5899 2	5899 2	5899 4	5899 2	—
Main jet	102	98	106	108	103	118	118	72
Pilot jet	45	45	50	48	48	45	45	40
Starter jet	50	50	50	50	50	50	50	50
Float (grams)	5	5	5	5	5	5	5	3·5
Air screw adjustment	$\frac{1}{2}$ turn	$\frac{1}{2}$ turn	$\frac{1}{2}$ turn	$\frac{1}{2}$ turn	$\frac{1}{2}$ turn	1–2 turns	1–2 turns	$\frac{3}{4}$ turn
Fitted to	150 SX	125 DL	175 Tv Series III	200 Tv	200 SX	150 GP	200 GP	J 125 J 125 Star-stream

9 Ignition and lighting—Li Models

FLYWHEEL magnetos fitted to all Li Series I and Series II models, and early Series III models, were of the four-pole generator type, and any one of four different makes—Dansi, Ducati, Filso or Marelli. As they differ in detail design it is important to specify the make when ordering spares

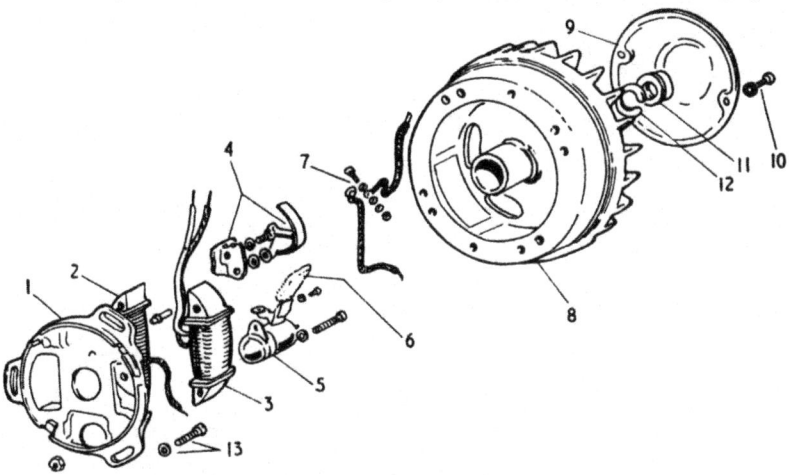

FIG. 40. FILSO FLYWHEEL-MAGNETO-GENERATOR

1. Stator plate
2. Ignition coil
3. Lighting coil
4. Contact-breaker assembly
5. Condenser
6. Felt pad
7. Terminal and wires
8. Flywheel
9. Dust cover
10. Screws fixing dust cover
11. Nut locking flywheel to shaft
12. Spring washer
13. Stator plate fixing-screws

as individual components are not generally interchangeable (or if they are, performance is reduced). This also applies to the (external) high-tension coil. The coil used with the Marelli magneto may be Marelli or Bosch and is different from the coil used with the Filso unit.

Only the Filso magneto is critical as regards the type of high-tension coil used (which should be Filso to provide a correct match). The Marelli and Ducati magnetos operate with equal efficiency on all coils. A Filso magneto (and coil) is virtually the standard for the Series I Tv 175; and the Ducati unit the standard for all Series II machines.

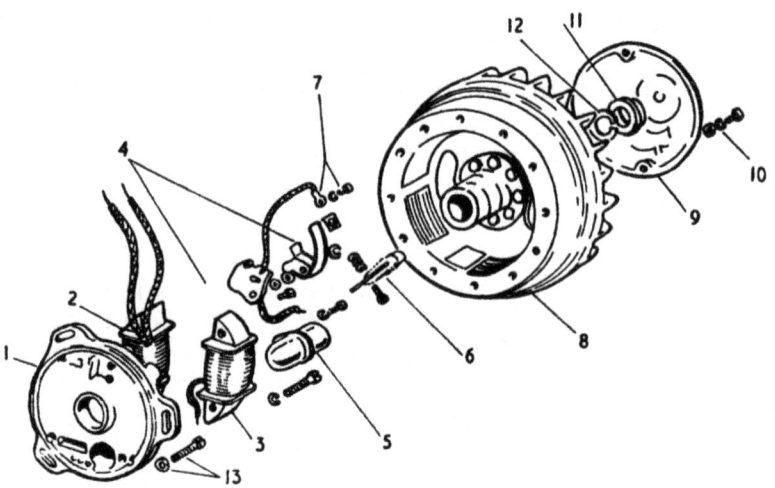

FIG. 41. MARELLI FLYWHEEL-MAGNETO-GENERATOR

1. Stator plate
2. Lighting coil
3. Ignition coil
4. Contact-breaker assembly
5. Condenser
6. Felt pad
7. Terminal

8. Flywheel
9. Dust cover
10. Screws for fixing dust cover
11. Nut locking flywheel to shaft
12. Spring washer
13. Stator plate fixing-screws

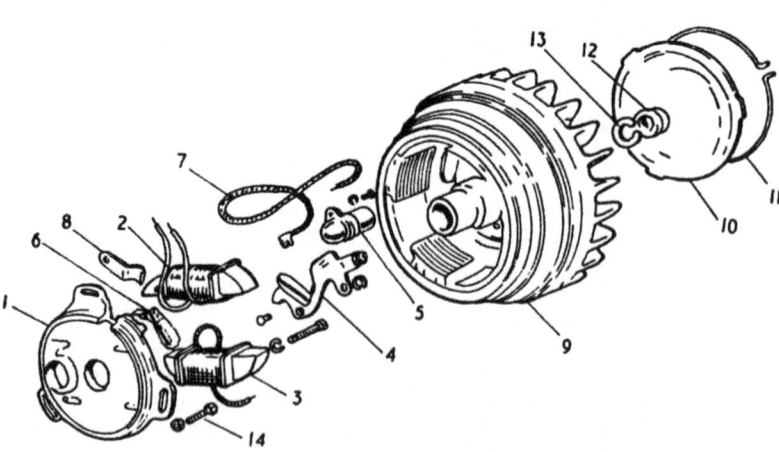

FIG. 42. DUCATI FLYWHEEL-MAGNETO-GENERATOR

1. Stator plate
2. Lighting coil
3. Ignition coil
4. Contact-breaker assembly
5. Condenser
6. Felt pad
7. Ignition cable

8. Plate fixing magneto wires
9. Flywheel
10. Dust cover
11. Spring clip retaining dust cover
12. Flywheel nut
13. Spring washer
14. Stator plate fixing-screws

Correct spark timing is established at 22–24° before top dead centre (T.D.C.), the factory setting of the stator plate being 23° before T.D.C., and this should not require altering. Geometrically this position is equivalent to the pole pieces of the magneto being equally spaced between the pole pieces of the coils 10° before ignition occurs, i.e. this alignment given 33° before T.D.C. If it is necessary to check the timing, or re-set, the recommended method is to mark the flywheel and housing adjacent to it to correspond with the T.D.C. position of the piston. The correct advance

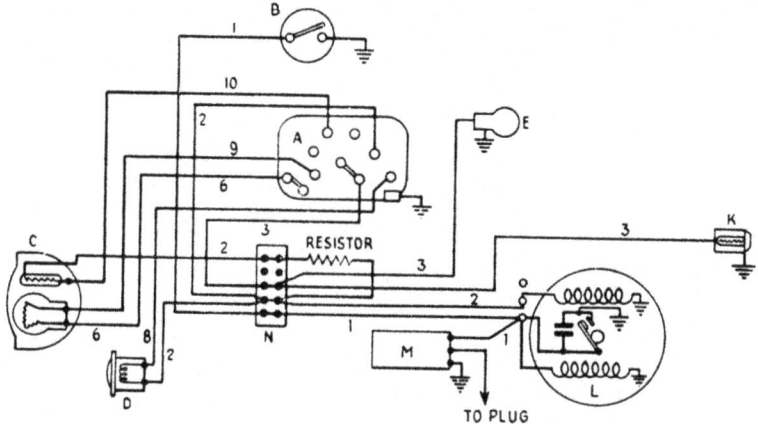

Fig. 43. Li 125 Series I Wiring Diagram Applicable
to Early Models

A. Main light switch
B. Press-button cut-off switch
C. Headlamp
D. Horn
E. Speedometer light bulb

K. Rear lamp
L. Flywheel magneto
M. Ignition coil
N. Terminal strip

Wiring colour code—

1. Green	6. Red
2. Brown	7. Purple
3. Black	8. White
4. Grey	9. Blue
5. Pink	10. Yellow

(23°) is then given by marking off a length of 1 3/16 in. along the housing in an anti-clockwise direction and rotating the flywheel in an anti-clockwise direction for the flywheel mark to line up (i.e. the flywheel is advanced 1 3/16 in. from the T.D.C. position).

Contact-breaker adjustment has been covered in Chapter 3. It should be noted that there is no fixed gap setting and adjustment aims simply at getting the points to just separate at the correct timing position. Increasing the gap in the open position will tend to advance the point of opening, and reducing the gap to retard the opening. A battery bulb and leads connected to earth and the green wire junction in the rectifier box will provide a visual indication of point opening, if necessary.

A further point in connexion with the Li flywheel magneto, compared with LD and earlier Lambretta models, is that direction of rotation is clockwise; hence timing adjustment is in the opposite sense. The external high-tension coil is mounted under the rear mudguard (top fairing).

On the lighting side, the output to the lights is about 27 watts, absorbed by a 24 watt headlamp bulb, a 3 watt tail-light bulb and the speedometer bulb and horn circuit. Li 150 models have a battery to operate parking

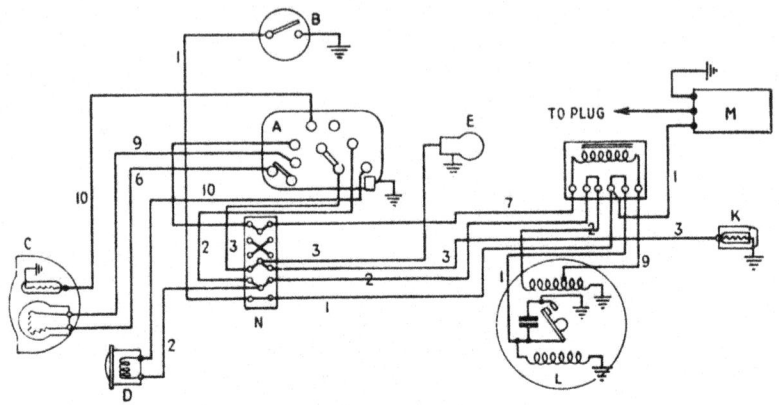

Fig. 44. Li 125 Later Series I and Series II Wiring Diagram
(*See* Fig. 43 for caption and colour code.)

lights, charged from the lighting output via a rectifier. Two different rates of charging are given, according to the position of the handlebar switch. For normal day running (all lights off—not when the headlamp, tail lamp and speedo lights are switched on for night driving), an impedance is switched into circuit for reducing the charging rate. On earlier models the impedance and fuse are mounted on the junction box behind the headlamp and on subsequent machines impedance, fuse and rectifier are mounted together in a square fitted to the left-hand footboard support arm. The respective wiring diagrams are shown in Figs. 43, 44, 45 and 46. Wiring is colour-coded for ease of identification and on the later models all three wires from the flywheel magneto go directly to the rectifier unit (green for ignition, brown for the main headlamp feed and blue for battery-charging current).

A stop-light can be fitted to the Li 150, although this is not standard practice, which utilizes the stop-light switch of the Tv 175 model and the appropriate lamp-housing for three bulbs. The additional wiring (corresponding to the pink lead on the Tv 175 circuit—*see* Fig. 46) runs from the stop switch to the rear lamps and from the stop switch to the grey lead on the junction box.

The Li 125 has no battery. On the first production models the magneto (lighting) output is fed direct to the bulbs and horn, the low light bulb being 12 volt, 10 watt. The appropriate wiring diagram is shown in Fig. 43. Later models have a revised switch and circuit, the magneto feeding the twin-filament headlamp bulb and horn only. The pilot light (6 volt, 5 watt) is fed through an impedance which regulates the magneto-current output. The rear light (and speedometer light bulb) is fed through the impedance in one switching position (pilot light and rear light on), or directly from the

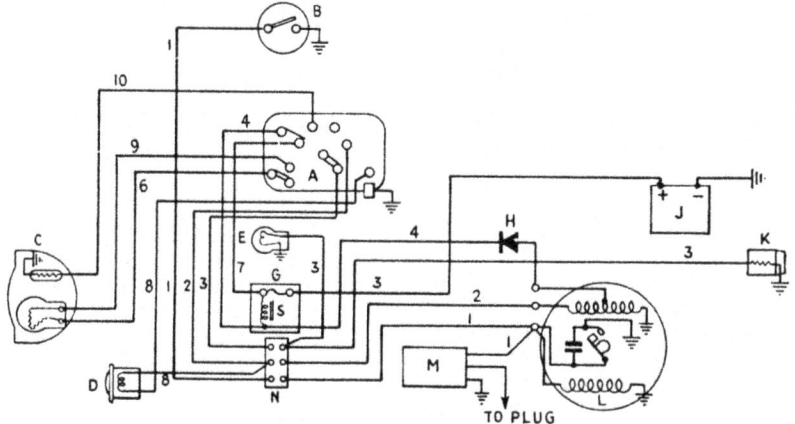

FIG. 45. LI 150 SERIES I WIRING DIAGRAM APPLICABLE
TO EARLY MODELS

H. Rectifier   G. Fuse
J. Battery   S. Choke coil
Other components as given in Fig. 43.

magneto when the headlamp is switched on. This wiring diagram is shown in Fig. 44.

A stop-light can be fitted to the original circuit. In this case the stop switch is wired to the two rear stop-lights, as above, and the other side to the purple wire on the junction box behind the headlamp.

Circuit testing should be quite straightforward, following the appropriate wiring diagrams. The main wiring from the handlebars is confined to a harness passing down by the front forks with separate wires to the headlamp assembly and horn (fully exposed by detaching the mudguard and headlamp casing). The battery is carried under the main cowling immediately in front of the tank, accessible by removal of the side panels. The rectifier box on the Li 150 is similarly exposed, on removal of the left-hand panel, mounted on the footboard support arm (although the fuse on the earlier models is mounted on the junction box behind the headlamp).

No fuse is used in the Li 125 circuit, nor a rectifier. A resistor on the

original circuit is mounted on the junction box behind the headlamp. On
the later models the impedance choke is separately mounted in a junction
box mounted on the left-hand footboard support arm (similar to the Li 150
but not containing a rectifier).

The light switch on all Li models is of the three-position type, marked
1, 0 and 2 (0 being the central position). The switch is mounted on the
right-hand side of the handlebars. A press-button in the centre of the
handlebars behind the steering head provides ignition cut-off for stopping
the engine by earthing the circuit. There is no ignition key or ignition

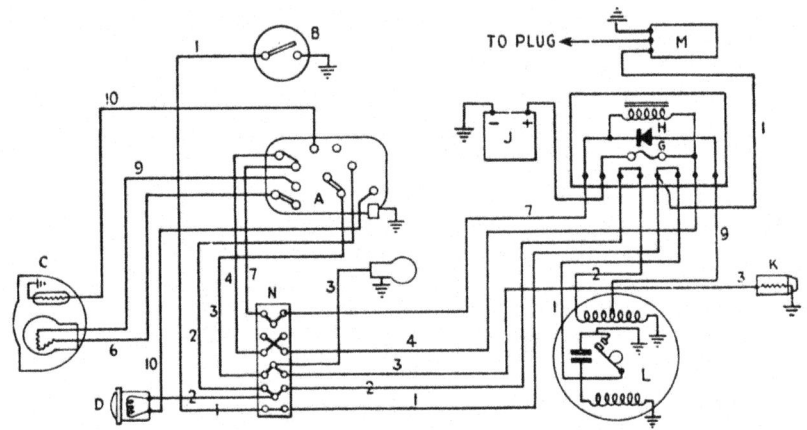

FIG. 46. Li 150 LATER SERIES I AND SERIES II WIRING DIAGRAM
(*See* Fig. 43 for key.)

switch but the Li 150 and all Series II models have a key-operated steering
lock.

Switch type may vary on different models but in all cases the central (O)
position corresponds to normal daytime driving with no lights. Position 1
(switch to the left) switches on the pilot light, rear and speedometer lights;
and position 2 (switch to the right) the headlamp, rear and speedometer
lights. Headlamp-dipping is accomplished by movement of the two-way
lever on the rear side of the switch-housing.

Charging current (where applicable) should be approximately 0·6 amp
at 3,000 r.p.m. and 1 amp at 5,000 r.p.m. and can be measured, if
necessary, by inserting an ammeter between the positive terminal of the
battery and the main circuit cable, i.e. disconnecting the battery at the
terminal and inserting the ammeter. Complete lack of charging current
(or failure of battery-operated lights to work) will normally be due to a
blown fuse.

(For care of battery and headlamp adjustment, *see* Chapter 10.)

TABLE 10
ELECTRICAL SPECIFICATION: LAMBRETTA Li 125
(see Figs. 43, 44)

Component	Type or Performance	Remarks
Flywheel-magneto .	Ducati, Filso or Marelli	
H.T. coil . .	Bosch, Ducati, Filso or Marelli	Filso coil goes only with Filso magneto.
Main switch . .	Three-position	Incorporates dip-switch and horn button.
Ignition cut-out .	Push-button switch	At centre of handlebars.
Headlamp bulb .	Twin filament 6 volt 25/25 watt	
Headlamp pilot bulb	6 volt 5 watt	12 volt 10 watt on original circuit (Fig. 43).
Rear light . .	6 volt 5 watt 6 volt 3 watt	No speedometer bulb. Where speedometer bulb and/ or stop-lights fitted.
Speedometer bulb .	12 volt 2·5 watt	If fitted, connects to black wire on headlamp junction box.

Note: If stop-lights are fitted an 18 ohm 5 watt resistor is also incorporated in the circuit and 6 volt 3 watt bulbs used throughout the tail-light group.

TABLE 11

ELECTRICAL SPECIFICATION: LAMBRETTA Li Models
(*see* Figs. 45, 46)

Component	Type or Performance	Remarks
Flywheel-magneto .	Ducati, Filso, or Marelli	
H.T. coil . .	Bosch, Ducati, Filso or Marelli	Coils interchangeable except that Filso coil can only be used with Filso magneto.
Rectifier* . .		Not interchangeable between the two different circuits.
Impedance choke* .	0·8 mH	On revised circuit.
Fuse* . . .	5 or 8 amps	
Horn* . . .	A.C.-operated	Non-adjustable.
Main switch . .	Three-position	Incorporates dip-switch and horn button.
Ignition cut-out .	Push-button switch	At centre of handlebars.
Headlamp bulb .	Twin filament 6 volt 25/25 watt	6 volt 3 watt on Li 150. 6 volt 5 watt where no speedometer bulb.
Headlamp pilot bulb	6 volt 5 watt	
Rear light . .	6 volt 3 watt	If fitted, connects to black wire on headlamp terminal block.
Speedometer bulb .	12 volt 2·5 watt	
Battery* . . .	6 volt 6·7 ampere-hour capacity.	

* Li 150 only.

Note: If stop-lights are fitted an 18 ohm 5 watt resistor is also incorporated in the circuit and 6 volt 3 watt bulbs used throughout the tail-light group.

10 Ignition and lighting—Tv Models

THE Tv electrical circuit differs from that of the Li models in that only the headlamp is fed direct from the flywheel magneto generator, whilst the pilot light, parking lights, stop-lights and also the horn are supplied with current from the battery. The rear light and speedometer bulb are fed

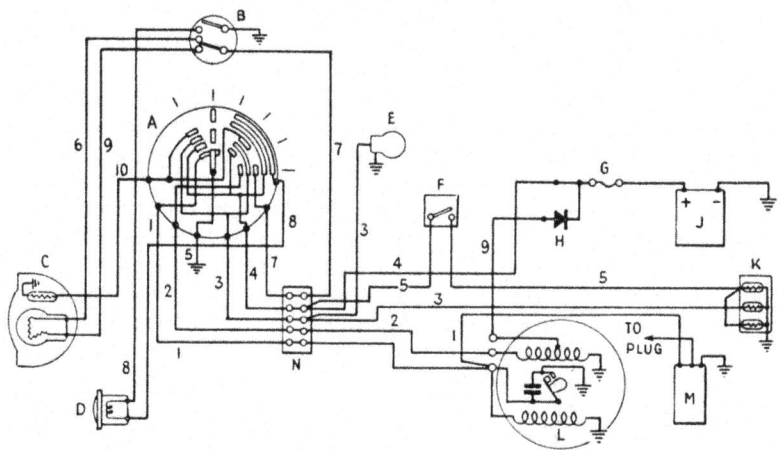

FIG. 47. EARLY TV 175 SERIES I WIRING DIAGRAM

A. Combined lighting and ignition switch
B. Handlebar switch (horn button and dip-switch)
C. Headlamp
D. Horn
E. Speedometer bulb
F. Stop-light switch
G. Fuse

H. Rectifier
J. Battery
K. Rear-lamp assembly
L. Flywheel magneto
M. Spark coil
N. Terminal block

(*See* Fig. 43 for wiring colour code.)

directly or from the battery according to the position of the main key-switch. Thus, unlike all other Lambretta models, the horn is battery-operated and independent of speed for response (and of effect on the lights). Stop-lights are a standard fitting and this circuit is independent of the main switching.

Again there are two different circuits. On the first series (*see* wiring diagram, Fig. 47) the rectifier is fed through an intermediate connexion of the lighting coil in all switch positions. On the later circuit (after engine No. 6102) the rectifier is fed in the same way in switch positions 0 and 2,

101

but in position 1 is fed through a relay switch so that an increase in charging rate is produced when the parking or "city driving" lights are switched on with the engine running. This relay switch is connected to the rear-lamp circuit and its operating position is governed by the current flowing in this circuit. When the relay is open (low current demand) charging current is drawn from the intermediate connexion on the lighting coil. When the relay is energized and closed (higher current demand) the connexion is now from the terminal or full-output end of the lighting coil. Component disposition, however, is the same on both versions, i.e. the fuse is always contained in the rectifier box positioned as on the Li models (this box also containing the relay on the later version).

Charging current is appreciably higher than on the Li 150, being approximately 1·5 amps at 4,000 r.p.m. and 3 amps at 6,000 r.p.m. on modified Tv Series I. The Tv Series II charging rate is the same as on Li Series II models.

The main switch is mounted in the centre of the handlebars and provides five switching positions, actuated by a key. The key can only be extracted in one position, corresponding to ignition "off" and lights out, i.e. "safe" daytime parking. With the key inserted and turned to the *left*, the battery operated lights are switched on for parking at night (pilot light, speedometer light and rear light). The *first* position to the *right* switches on the ignition for daytime riding; the *second* position to the *right* switches on the headlamp pilot light, rear light and speedometer light for "city" night driving; and the *third* or farthest position to the *right* switches on the headlamp for normal night driving. In all the right-hand switching positions the ignition is "on" and the horn circuit is connected to the battery (although "open" until the horn button is depressed). The stop-switch provides the only break on the stop-light circuit which is picked up on the main battery lead at the junction box (grey wire) and thence back to the stop-lights through the stop-switch. The two-way switch which controls the headlamp dip is mounted on the right-hand handlebar near the twist grip, the housing also accommodating the horn button.

A Filso flywheel magneto is standard on the Series I Tv 175, but different in detail from the one employed on the Li models, and not interchangeable. The coil is separately mounted in a similar position to the Li models. Correct timing position is 26–28 degrees before T.D.C., corresponding to an angular rotation in a clockwise direction of the flywheel (for point-opening) of $1\frac{8}{32}$ in. (32–3 mm) from T.D.C. position. (*see* description of Li magneto-timing adjustment).

The battery on the Series I Tv 175 is of 6·7 ampere-hour capacity. It is connected negative to earth and, if removed from the machine for any reason, care should be taken to ensure that it is always reconnected the right way round. Battery care is straightforward and consists mainly of never letting the battery dry out and never letting it run down completely. Topping-up with distilled water is normally called for at 4–6 week intervals (or half this figure in warm summer weather) so that the plates and separators remain just covered.

The condition of the battery is best checked with a hydrometer which records the specific gravity of the electrolyte, either with coloured-ball indicators or directly. In the latter case a charged battery should register a specific-gravity figure of 1·26. Any reading below about 1·22 indicates that the battery is in a "flat" state and calls for recharging. If the battery was not subjected to known excessive use, look for a reason why it has become discharged, e.g. lack of charging current, stop-light switch sticking on, or a long period of idleness or drying out, letting the battery deteriorate. If the machine is to be laid up it is always best to remove the battery, get it charged, as necessary, to full strength and recharge from

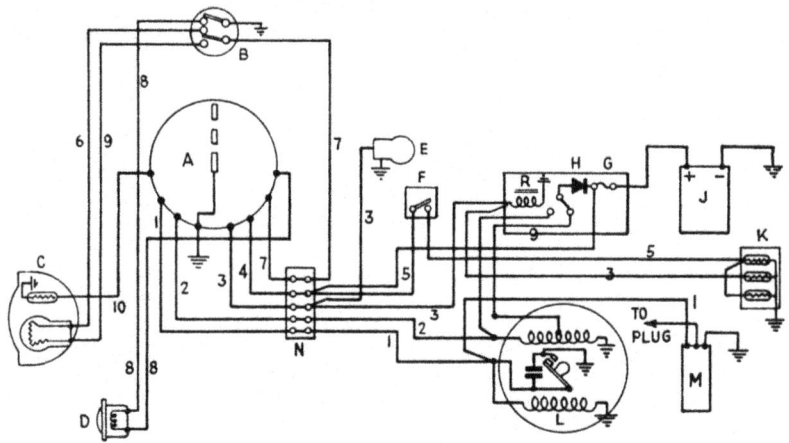

FIG. 48. LATER SERIES I AND ALL SERIES II TV 175
WIRING DIAGRAM
R. Relay
Other components are given in the key to Fig. 47.

time to time to prevent deterioration. Permanent damage to the plates can result if the battery is left in a discharged condition, or allowed to dry out.

Recommended charging current for recharging, where a home-charger unit is available, is one tenth of the ampere-hour capacity, e.g. 0·7 amp with the Tv 175 battery. The same figure is applicable to the Li Series batteries. Charging *time* will be somewhat longer than the 10 hours apparently required and can be continued for a further 2–3 hours after each individual cell shows 2·6 volts on open circuit, i.e. as read by a voltmeter connected directly across the cell terminals.

Headlamp adjustment is identical on all models. The two screws marked V on the headlamp can be loosened when the lamp can be inclined to raise or lower the beam. The correct setting is established by placing the machine on a level 16–17 feet away from a suitable vertical surface on which a mark has been made 30 in. above ground-level height. The machine should have tyre pressures correct and be mounted with its normal load, i.e. the rider sitting in position and with both wheels on the ground, not on its stand. The headlamp setting should then be adjusted so that in the "dip" position the top of the beam just comes level with the 30 in. mark.

TABLE 12

ELECTRICAL SPECIFICATION: LAMBRETTA Tv 175

(*see* Figs. 47, 48)

Component	Type or Performance	Remarks
Flywheel-magneto .	Filso (Series I) Ducati (Series II)	
H. T. coil . .	Filso or Bosch	Externally fitted.
Rectifier and fuse .	(Original circuit)	Rectifier current 0·5 amps Fuse 5 or 8 amps.
Rectifier-fuse-relay .	(Modified circuit)* (Maximum setting)	Rectifier current 1·5 amps Fuse 5 or 8 amps.
Horn . . .	6 volt D.C.	Battery-operated, adjustable by set-screw in back centre of handlebars.
Main switch . .	Five-position	
Secondary switch .	Headlamp dip and horn button	On right-hand handlebar.
Headlamp bulb .	Twin filament 6 volt 25/25 watt	
Headlamp pilot-bulb	6 volt 5 watt (festoon)	39 mm long.
Rear light . .	6 volt 3 watt (festoon)	
Stop-lights . .	Two 6 volt 3 watt (festoon).	30 mm long.
Speedometer bulb .	12 volt 2·5 watt	
Battery . . .	6 volt 6·7 ampere-hour capacity	Series I and Series II.

* *Note.* The Tv Series II model is the same as for the Li Series II models.

11 Ignition and lighting—Series III Models

FROM 1962 onwards ignition and lighting has been provided by a six-pole generator, made only by Dansi or Ducati. This was fitted from the following frame numbers onwards—

Li 125–36626
Li 150–631475
Tv 175–507945

TABLE 13
BULB SIZES—SERIES III 125 AND 150
(For machines with and without Batteries)*

Bulb	Specification	Type	Socket
Headlamp . .	6 volt 25/25 watt	Spherical	BA 20d
Headlamp pilot light	6 volt 5 watt	Festoon	S 8·5/9·5
Speedometer . .	12 volt 2·5 watt	Cylindrical	BA 9s
Rear light . .	6 volt 3/15 watt	Spherical	BAY 15d/19

* *Note.* For machines with Battery—Fuse 8 amp, Battery 8 ampere-hour.

TABLE 14
BULB SIZES—SERIES III 175 AND GT 200; 150 SX AND 200 SX

Bulb	Specification	Type	Socket
Headlamp . .	6 volt 25/25 watt	Spherical	BA 20d
Headlamp pilot light	6 volt 5 watt	Festoon	S 8·5/9·5
Speedometer . .	12 volt 3 watt	Spherical	BA 9s
Rear light . .	6 volt 3/15 watt	Spherical	BAY 15d/19

Note. Fuse 8 amp. Battery 8 ampere-hour.

105

The six-pole generators can be identified by the fact that the rectifier has a black plastic cover. Internally it can be recognized by having five coils on the stator plate, whereas the four-pole generators have only two coils. Six-pole generators were also fitted to later models without battery, in which case the coils and circuitry differ. These models are the Li 150, Li 150 Special and SX 150 with direct lighting (no battery) system. All the J range models also have direct lighting (no battery), and in this case a Ducati six-pole generator is fitted, but smaller in dimensions than on the other models.

The following modifications and production changes should also be noted.

Early six-pole generator units employed a flywheel with brass ribs and a separate fan ring riveted in place. This was replaced with the introduction of the SX series by a one-piece diecast unit. A later modification was to increase the diameter of the hub from 27 mm to 28 mm. Only 28 mm hub sizes are available as standard replacements and if fitted to an earlier model generator the inside diameter of the stator plate must be lathe turned to a diameter of 29 mm to match. The fitting of a new flywheel also requires the use of a new type nut and washer as the boss shape is slightly different.

If a new flywheel is fitted as a replacement for an early brass type the higher current generated may cause trouble by blowing light bulbs. To avoid changing the coils, a much less expensive cure can be carried out by fitting a "Clipper Diode" wired in parallel with the black wire in the tail lamp housing.

All the 6 volt lighting systems are negative earth.

12 VOLT LIGHTING SYSTEMS

A 12 volt lighting conversion set was introduced for Li models in 1964, intended to convert any existing machine to 12 volt operation. This comprises a rewired stator assembly, a new rectifier and fuse, and a zener diode and heat sink. Associated with this are a new 12 volt battery, and new 12 volt bulbs. It should be noted that conversion can only be applied to six-pole generators, and is specifically intended for the Li models. It can, however, be adapted to convert J range models with direct lighting system. In this case two extra coils have to be changed on the stator.

Full details for conversion are supplied with the kits. The 12 volt system has reversed earth connexion compared with the original system, i.e. is positive earth.

WIRING CIRCUITS

Similar general notes on ignition and wiring, etc., apply as for the previous models (Chapters 9 and 10), although the wiring circuits are different. The terminal strip employed on all earlier models is eliminated and the main wiring harness terminates on a block in the headlamp assembly.

Appropriate data for servicing, etc., are given in the following wiring diagrams and tables.

The six-pole flywheel magneto has a rated output of 27 watts. The armature winding consists of five coils, three of which are independent and two are connected in series. In machines without battery the three independent coils feed the ignition circuit (green), driving light (violet) and stop light (rose). The two series connected coils feed the horn circuit and the high and low headlight beam circuit.

TABLE 15

BULB SIZES—12. J SERIES

Bulb	Specification	Type	Socket
Headlamp . .	6 volt 25/25 watt	Spherical	BA 20d
Pilot light and speedometer .	6 volt 5 watt	Festoon	S 8·5/9·5
Rear light . .	6 volt 3/15 watt	Spherical	BAY 15d/19

Head- and tail-lamps may be made by Aprillia, Carello or CEV, and components from each are not interchangeable. There may also be differences in the actual equipment and wiring.

Li 125 and Li 150 models have headlamps which can be adjusted by slackening the three retaining screws on the front rim and then rotating the complete unit. The Li 150 Special, SX 150 and larger models have a headlamp with a hexagonal rim, secured by four screws. Headlamp adjustment is by means of a central screw, located below the lamp. The GP models have a rectangular headlamp, also with a single screw for adjustment.

J series models use headlamps by either Aprillia or CEV, with beam adjustments as for the Li 125 and Li 150 models.

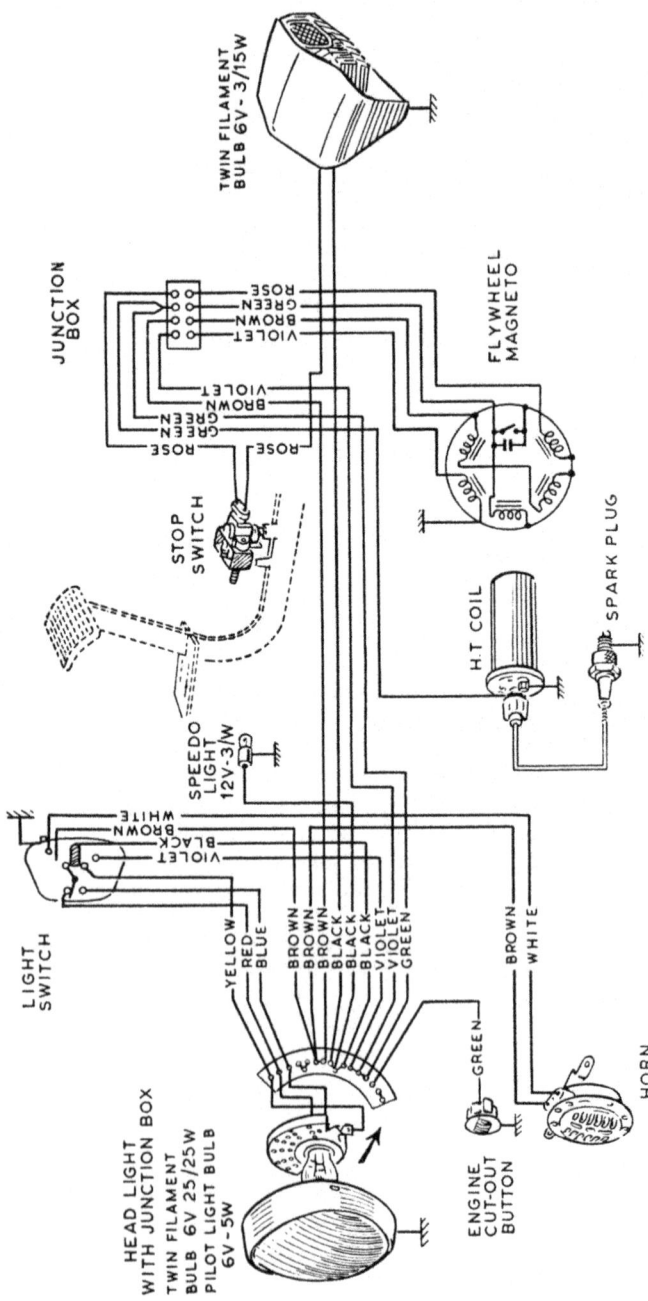

TWIN FILAMENT
BULB 6V - 3/15W

JUNCTION
BOX

ROSE
GREEN
BROWN
VIOLET

FLYWHEEL
MAGNETO

VIOLET
BROWN
GREEN
GREEN
ROSE   ROSE

SPARK PLUG

STOP
SWITCH

H.T. COIL

SPEEDO
LIGHT
12V-3/W

WHITE
BROWN
BLACK
VIOLET

LIGHT
SWITCH

YELLOW
RED
BLUE
BROWN
BROWN
BROWN
BLACK
BLACK
BLACK
VIOLET
VIOLET
GREEN

BROWN
WHITE

HEAD LIGHT
WITH JUNCTION BOX
TWIN FILAMENT
BULB 6V 25/25W
PILOT LIGHT BULB
6V - 5W

GREEN

ENGINE
CUT-OUT
BUTTON

HORN

FIG. 49. WIRING DIAGRAM FOR THE SERIES III 125 AND 150 C.C. (MACHINES WITHOUT BATTERY)

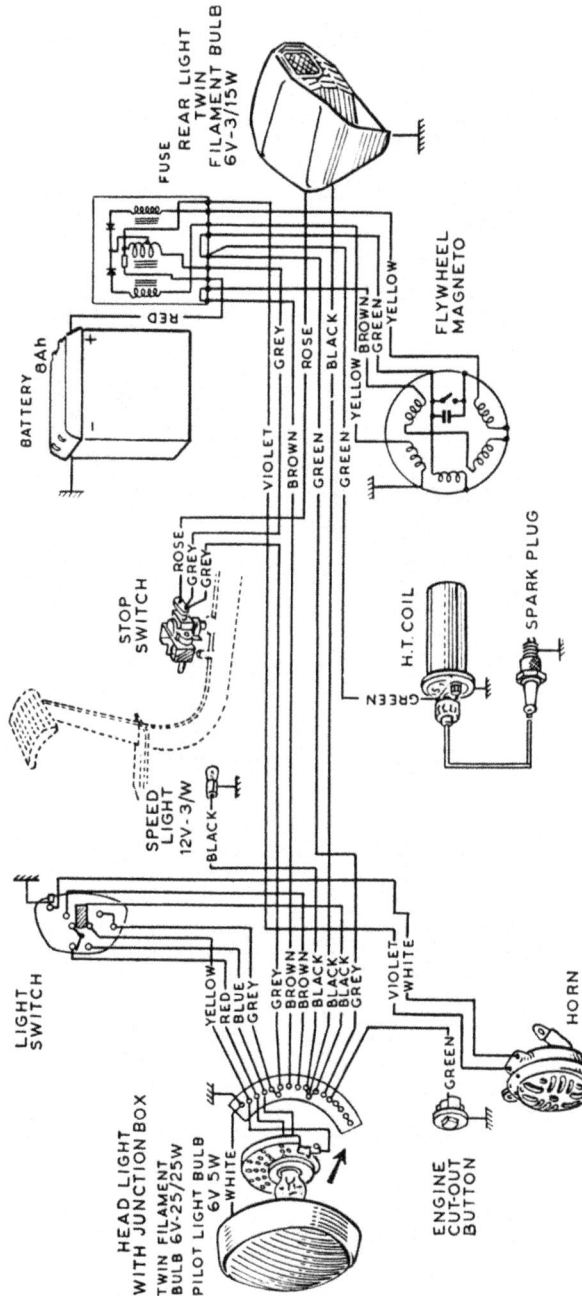

FIG. 50. WIRING DIAGRAM FOR THE SERIES III 125 AND 150 C.C. (MACHINES WITH BATTERY)

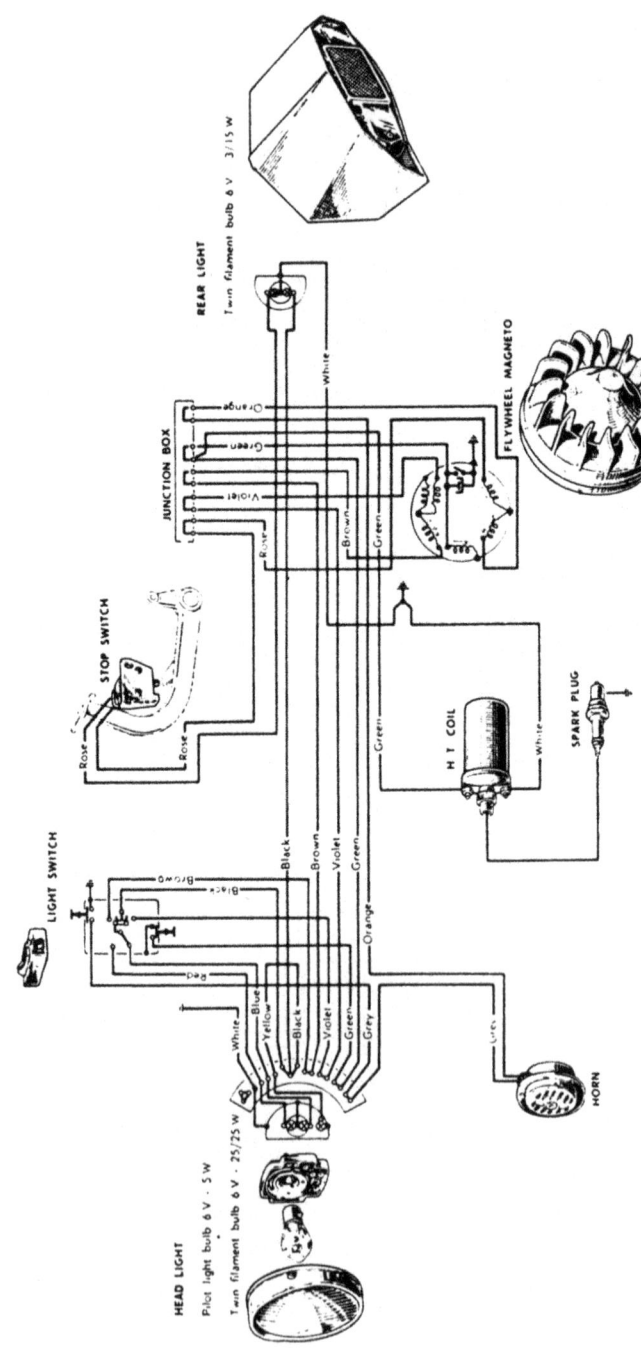

REAR LIGHT

Twin filament bulb 6 V   3/15 w

FLYWHEEL MAGNETO

JUNCTION BOX

Orange

Green

Violet

Rose

Brown

Green

STOP SWITCH

Rose

Rose

White

SPARK PLUG

H T COIL

White

Green

LIGHT SWITCH

Black

Brown

Black

Black

Brown

Violet

Green

Orange

Red

White

Blue

Yellow

Black

Violet

Green

Grey

Green

HORN

HEAD LIGHT

Pilot light bulb 6 V · 5 w

Twin filament bulb 6 V · 25/25 w

Fig. 51. Wiring Diagram for the J Series 125

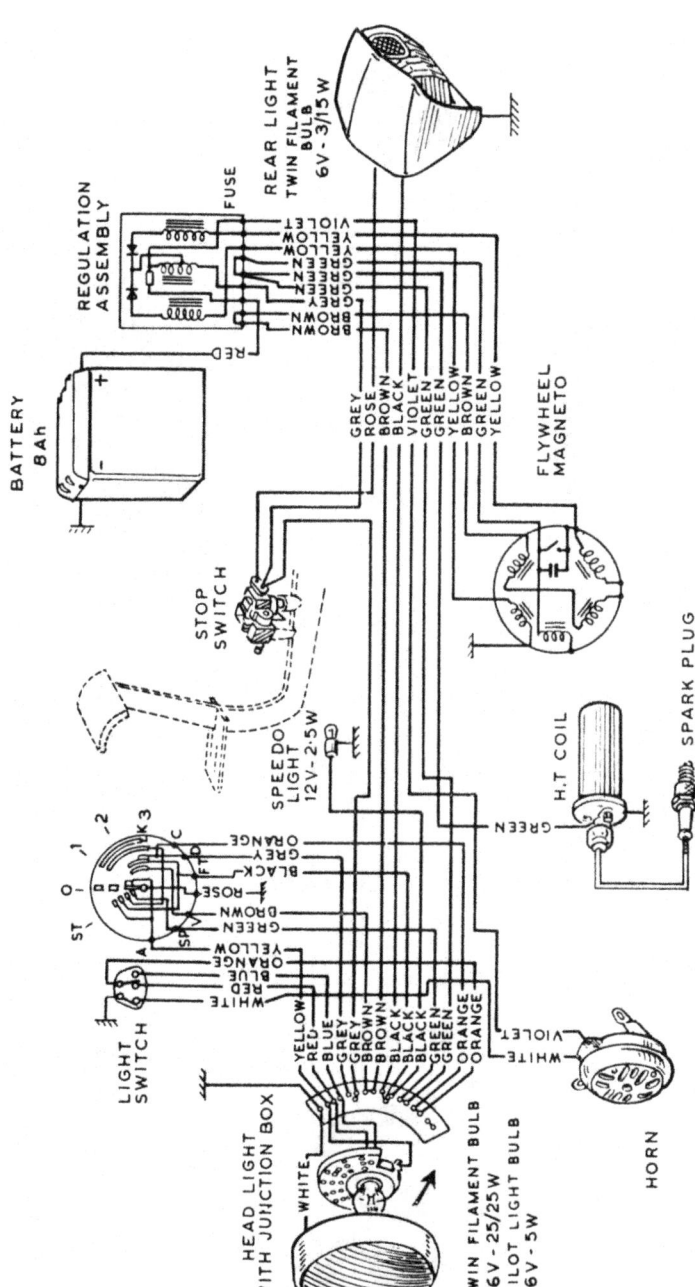

Fig. 52. Wiring Diagram for the Series III 175 c.c., GT 200, and 200 SX

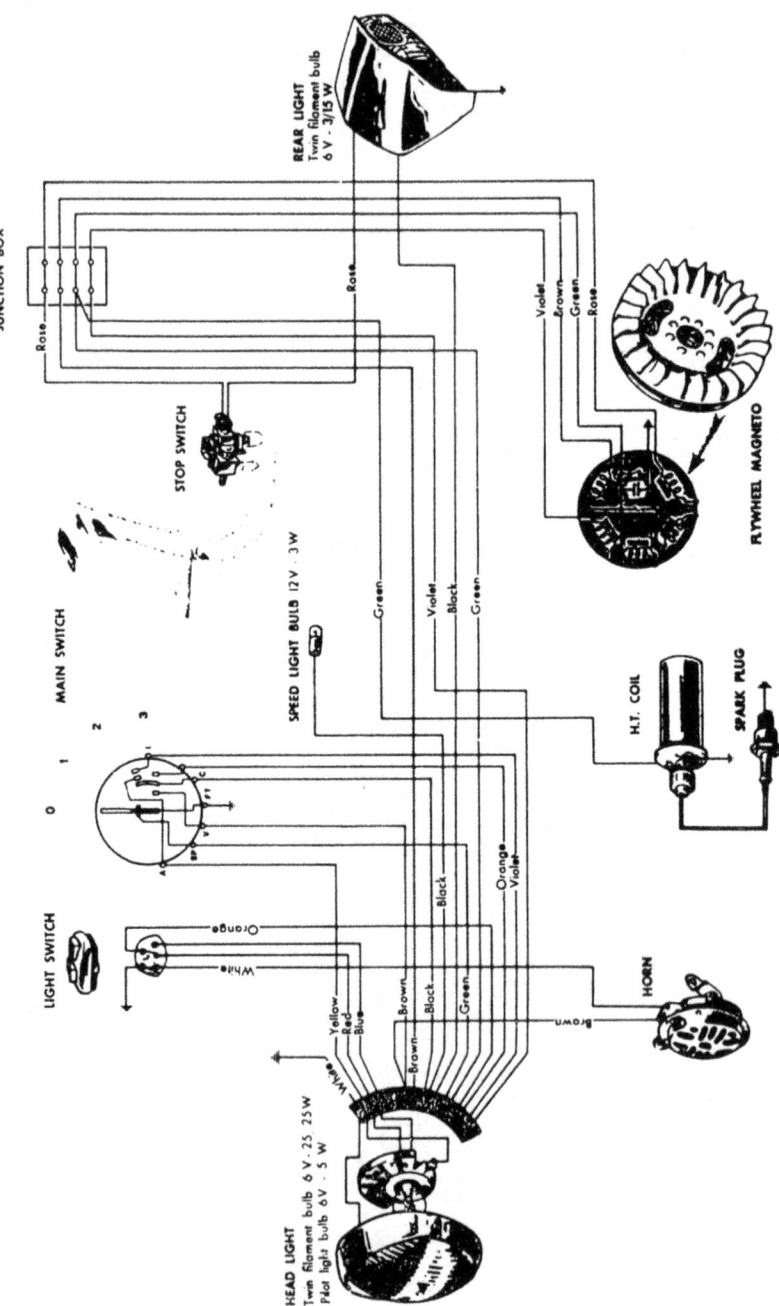

FIG. 53. WIRING DIAGRAM FOR THE SX 150 WITHOUT BATTERY

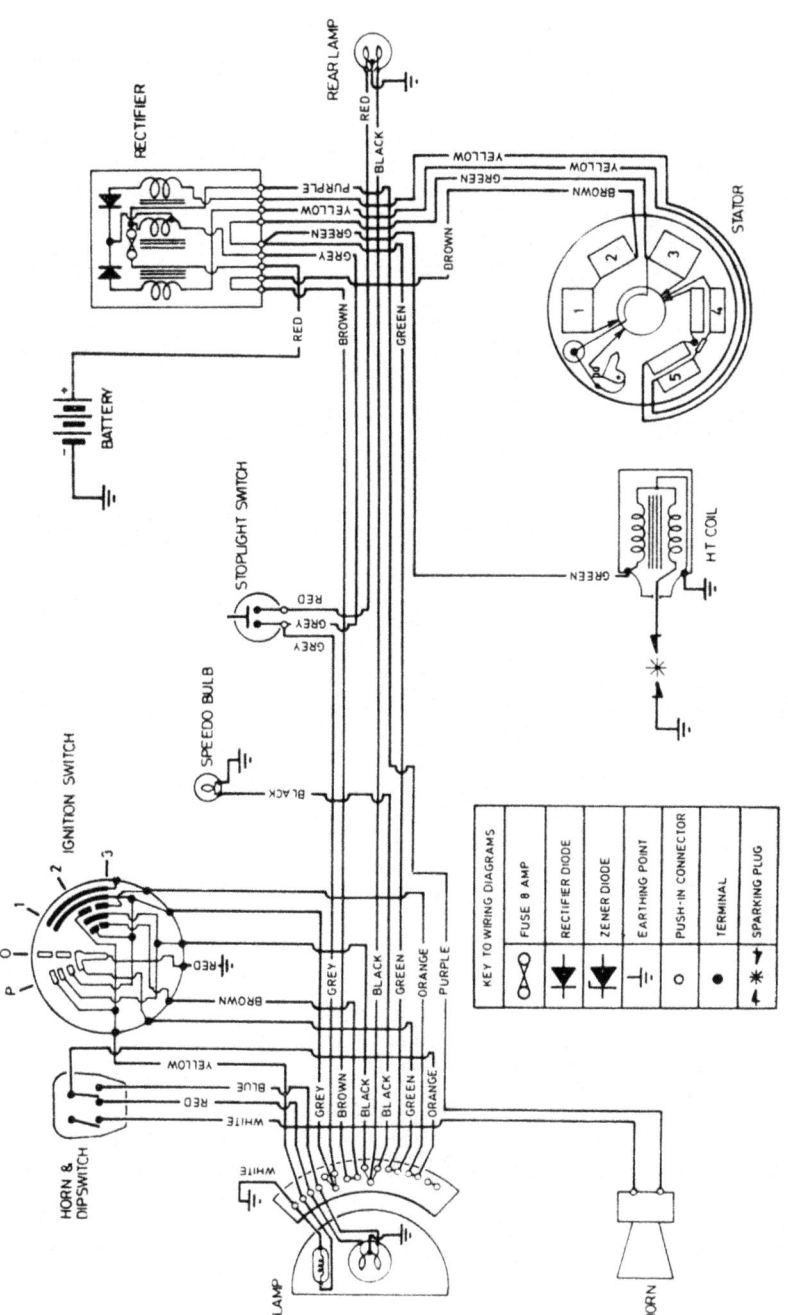

Fig. 54. Wiring Diagram for Tv Series III, Li 150 S, SX 150, GP 150, GP 200, GT 200 and SX 200

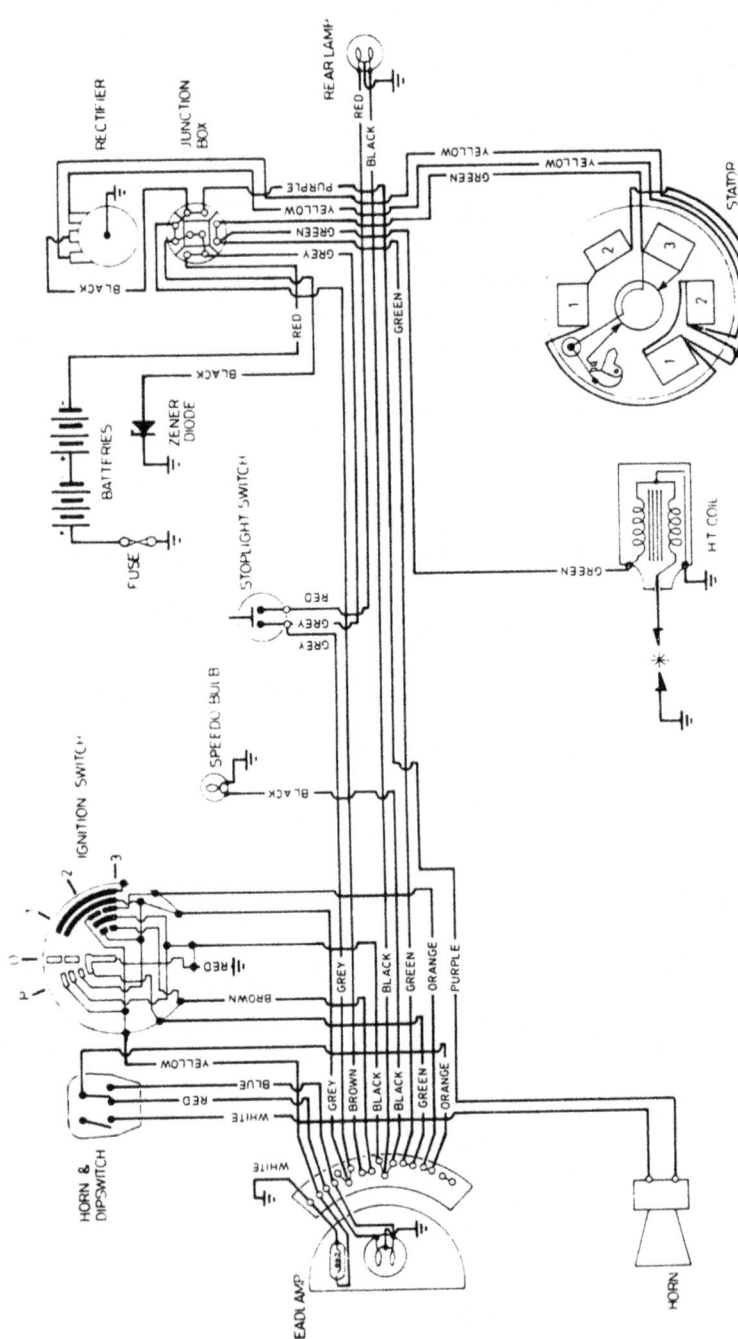

Fig. 55. 12 Volt Conversion for Use with Six-pole Generators

Appendix—Summary of Dimensions and Tolerances

Li 125 CYLINDER AND PISTON DIMENSIONS (All dimensions in millimetres)

Grade		Cylinder		Piston	
		Dia.	Tolerance	Dia.	Tolerance
Standard	−	52·0	+ 0·006	51·9	+ 0·058 + 0·064
	0	52·0	+ 0·007 + 0·013	51·9	+ 0·065 + 0·071
	+	52·0	+ 0·014 + 0·020	51·9	+ 0·072 + 0·078
First Oversize	−	52·2	+ 0·006	52·1	+ 0·058 + 0·064
	0	52·2	+ 0·007 + 0·013	52·1	+ 0·065 + 0·071
	+	52·2	+ 0·014 + 0·020	52·1	+ 0·072 + 0·078
Second Oversize	−	52.4	+ 0·006	52·3	+ 0·058 + 0·064
	0	52·4	+ 0·007 + 0·013	52·3	+ 0·065 + 0·071
	+	52·4	+ 0·014 + 0·020	52·3	+ 0·072 + 0·078
Third Oversize	−	52·6	+ 0·006	52·5	+ 0·058 + 0·064
	0	52·6	+ 0·007 + 0·013	52·5	+ 0·065 + 0·071
	+	52·6	+ 0·014 + 0·020	52·5	+ 0·072 + 0·078

Wear limit: 0·15 mm on diameter in all cases.
Assembly tolerance: 0·036 mm minimum, 0·048 mm maximum.

LI 150 CYLINDER AND PISTON DIMENSIONS
(All dimensions in millimetres)

Grade		Cylinder		Piston	
		Dia.	Tolerance	Dia.	Tolerance
Standard	−	57·0	+ 0·006	56·9	+ 0·060 + 0·066
	0	57·0	+ 0·007 + 0·013	56·9	+ 0·067 + 0·073
	+	57·0	+ 0·014 + 0·020	56·9	+ 0·074 + 0·080
First Oversize	−	57·2	+ 0·006	57·1	+ 0·060 + 0·066
	0	57·2	+ 0·007 + 0·013	57.1	+ 0·067 + 0·073
	+	57·2	+ 0·014 + 0·020	57·1	+ 0·074 + 0·080
Second Oversize	−	57·4	+ 0·006	57·3	+ 0·060 + 0·066
	0	57·4	+ 0·007 + 0·013	57·3	+ 0·067 + 0·073
	+	57·4	+ 0·014 + 0·020	57·3	+ 0·074 + 0·080
Third Oversize	−	57·6	+ 0·006	57·5	+ 0·060 + 0·066
	0	57·6	+ 0·007 + 0·013	57·5	+ 0·067 + 0·073
	+	57·6	+ 0·014 + 0·020	57·5	+ 0·074 + 0·080

Wear limit: 0·15 mm on diameter in all cases.
Assembly tolerance: 0·036 mm minimum, 0·046 mm maximum.

Tv 175 Series I Cylinder and Piston Dimensions
(All dimensions in millimetres)

Grade		Cylinder		Piston	
		Dia.	Tolerance	Dia. (at bottom groove)	Tolerance
Standard	−	60·0	+ 0·006	59·8	+ 0·045 + 0·051
	0	60·0	+ 0·007 + 0·013	59·8	+ 0·052 + 0·058
	+	60·0	+ 0·014 + 0·020	59·8	+ 0·059 + 0·065
First Oversize	−	60·2	+ 0·006	60·0	+ 0·045 + 0·051
	0	60·2	+ 0·007 + 0·013	60·0	+ 0·052 + 0·058
	+	60·2	+ 0·014 + 0·020	60·0	+ 0·059 + 0·065
Second Oversize	−	60·4	+ 0·006	60·2	+ 0·045 + 0·051
	0	60·4	+ 0·007 + 0·013	60·2	+ 0·052 + 0·058
	+	60·4	+ 0·014 + 0·020	60·2	+ 0·059 + 0·065
Third Oversize	−	60·6	+ 0·006	60·4	+ 0·045 + 0·051
	0	60·6	+ 0·007 + 0·013	60·4	+ 0·052 + 0·058
	+	60·6	+ 0·014 + 0·020	60·4	+ 0·059 + 0·065

(Rebored — indicated along the Second and Third Oversize cylinder diameters)

Wear limit: 0·18 mm on diameter in all cases.
Assembly tolerance: 0·044 mm minimum, 0·056 mm maximum.

Note: Series II Tv 175 similar except that diameter sizes are—
Cylinder—62·0, 62·2, 62·4 and 62·6 mm
Piston—61·8, 62·0, 62·2 and 62·4 mm

PISTON-RING AND GROOVE DIMENSIONS (ALL MODELS)
(All dimensions in millimetres)

	Groove		Ring		Assembly Tolerance
	Width	Tolerance	Thickness	Tolerance	
Top groove .	2·5	+ 0·050 + 0·075	2·5	0 − 0·025	0·05–0·10
Bottom groove	2·5	+ 0·040 + 0·065	2·5	0 − 0·025	0·04–0·09

Wear limit: 0·2 mm

BIG-END DIMENSIONS (ALL MODELS)
(All dimensions in millimetres)

	Crankshaft pin		Connecting rod		Assembly Tolerance
	Width	Tolerance	Width	Tolerance	
Standard . .	14·0	0 − 0·110	13·8	− 0·032 − 0·075	0·122–0·275

Wear limit: 0·4 mm

Index

OTHER MOTORCYCLE MANUALS AVAILABLE IN THIS SERIES

AJS (BOOK OF) ALL MODELS 1955-1965:
350cc & 500cc Singles ~ Models 16,16S,18, 18S

ARIEL WORKSHOP MANUAL 1933-1951:
All single, twin & 4 cylinder models

ARIEL (BOOK OF) MAINTENANCE & REPAIR MANUAL 1932-1939:
LF3, LF4, LG, NF3, NF4, NG, OG, VA, VA3, VA4, VB, VF3, VF4, VG, Red Hunter LH, NH, OH, VH & Square Four 4F, 4G, 4H

BMW FACTORY WORKSHOP MANUAL R27, R28:
English, German, French and Spanish text

BMW FACTORY WORKSHOP MANUAL R50, R50S, R60, R69S:
Also includes a supplement for the USA models: R50US, R60US, R69US. English, German, French and Spanish text

BSA PRE-WAR SINGLES & TWINS (BOOK OF) 1936-1939:
All Pre-War single & twin cylinder SV & OHV models through 1939
150cc, 250cc, 350cc, 500cc, 600cc, 750cc & 1,000cc

BSA SINGLES (BOOK OF) 1945-1954:
OHV & SV 250cc, 350cc, 500cc & 600cc, Groups B, C & M

BSA SINGLES (BOOK OF) 1955-1967:
B31, B32, B33, B34 and "Star" B40 & SS90

BSA 250cc SINGLES (BOOK OF) 1954-1970:
B31, B32, B33, B34 and "Star" B40 & SS90

BSA TWINS (BOOK OF) 1948-1962:
All 650cc & 500cc twins

BSA TWINS (SECOND BOOK OF) 1962-1969:
All 650cc & 500cc, A50 & A65 OHV unit construction twins

DUCATI OHC FACTORY WORKSHOP MANUAL:
160 Junior Monza, 250 Monza, 250 GT, 250 Mark 3, 250 Mach 1, 250 SCR & 350 Sebring

HONDA 250 & 305cc FACTORY WORKSHOP MANUAL:
C.72 C.77 CS.72, CS.77, CB.72, CB.77 [HAWK]

HONDA 125 & 150cc FACTORY WORKSHOP MANUAL:
C.92, CS.92, CB.92, C.95 & CA.95

HONDA 90 (BOOK OF) ALL MODELS UP TO 1966:
All 90cc variations including the S90, CM90, C200, S65, Trail 90 & C65 models

HONDA 50cc FACTORY WORKSHOP MANUAL: C.100

HONDA 50cc FACTORY WORKSHOP MANUAL: C.110

HONDA (BOOK OF) MAINTENANCE & REPAIR 1960-1966:
50cc C.100, C.102, C.110 & C.114 ~ 125cc C.92 & CB.92
250cc C.72 & CB.72 ~ 305cc CB.77

LAMBRETTA (BOOK OF) MAINTENANCE & REPAIR:
125 & 150cc, all models up to 1958, except model "48".

LAMBRETTA (SECOND BOOK OF) MAINTENANCE & REPAIR:
125, 150, 175 & 200cc, all Li & TV models and derivates from 1958 to 1970.

**NORTON FACTORY TWIN CYLINDER WORKSHOP MANUAL
1957-1970:** *Lightweight Twins:* 250cc Jubilee, 350cc Navigator and 400cc
Electra and the *Heavyweight Twins:* Model 77, 88, 88SS, 99, 99SS, Sports
Special, Manxman, Mercury, Atlas, G15, P11, N15, Ranger (P11A).

NORTON (BOOK OF) MAINTENANCE & REPAIR 1932-1939:
All Pre-War SV, OHV and OHC models: 16H, 16I, 18, 19, 20, 50, 55, ES2,
CJ, CSI, International 30 & 40

SUZUKI 200 & 250cc FACTORY WORKSHOP MANUAL:
250cc T20 [X-6 Hustler] ~ 200cc T200 [X-5 Invader & Sting Ray Scrambler]

SUZUKI 250cc FACTORY WORKSHOP MANUAL: 250cc ~ T10

TRIUMPH (BOOK OF) MAINTENANCE & REPAIR 1935-1939:
All Pre-War single & twin cylinder models: L2/1, 2/1, 2/5, 3/1, 3/2, 3/5, 5/1,
5/2, 5/3, 5/4, 5/5, 5/10, 6/1, Tiger 70, 80, 90 & 2H. Tiger 70C, 3S & 3H,
Tiger 80C & 5H, Tiger 90C, 6S, 2HC & 3SC, 5T & 5S and T100

TRIUMPH 1937-1951 WORKSHOP MANUAL (A. St. J. Masters):
Covers rigid frame and sprung hub single cylinder SV & OHV and twin
cylinder OHV pre-war, military, and post-war models

TRIUMPH 1945-1955 FACTORY WORKSHOP MANUAL NO.11:
Covers pre-unit, twin-cylinder rigid frame, sprung hub, swing-arm and 350cc,
500cc & 650cc.

VELOCETTE (BOOK OF) MAINTENANCE & REPAIR:
Covers LE Mk. I, II, & III, Valiant, Vogue, MOV, MAC, KSS, KTS, Viper,
Venom & Thruxton. Includes some limited material on the Viceory scooter

VESPA (BOOK OF) MAINTENANCE & REPAIR 1946-1959:
All 125cc & 150cc models including 42/L2 & Gran Sport

VINCENT WORKSHOP MANUAL 1935-1955:
All Series A, B & C Models